SEVEN STEPS TO RIGHT THINKING

A THOUGHTFUL SYSTEM FOR HEALING

Beca Lewis

Seven Steps To Right Thinking is published by:
Perception Publishing

This book is part of *The Shift Series*

Original Copyright ©2003 by Beca Lewis

Cover Design: Elizabeth Mackey

The Seven Steps To Right Thinking
Copyright©2020. All rights reserved.

No part of this book may be reproduced or transmitted in any form or by any means, electronic or mechanical, including photocopying, recording or by any information storage and retrieval system, without written permission from the author, except for the inclusion of brief quotations in a review.

ISBN-13: 978-0-9885520-9-8

Beca's Website: *becalewis.com*

WHAT OTHERS SAY ABOUT THIS BOOK

I have read several of Beca's books and taken many of her classes. Each one gets better and better as I grow and begin to understand my spiritual journey. The Right Thinking book was one of my favorites. While perfect at any stage of your life, it helped me start the transition from working to retirement. For a person who has worked all her life and loves her career, the idea of retirement was scary. I felt like I would be losing my identity. In the end, I was able to realize that my life's purpose did not stop at retirement. I am now enjoying my next stage of life. Thank you, Beca!!!! —Patricia Kearney

Whether you take it with a group or read the book on your own, this course is so helpful if you are like me. I tend to overthink things, so I need simple, practical guidelines for any learning process, especially in the spiritual arena. Beca took me through all the steps, in sequence, helping me to build a solid foundation on which to ground myself and live a much more graceful life—a life of truly Right Thinking! —Jet Tucker

TABLE OF CONTENTS

Preface	5
Chapter One: Preparing	6
Chapter Two: Perception	14
Chapter Three: Your Way	20
Chapter Four: Begin	25
Chapter Five: You First	33
Chapter Six: Intent	40
Shifting Our Point of View	*42*
Shifting Our State of Mind	*43*
Practical Intent	*48*
Chapter Seven: Premise	51
Face And Replace: I choose Sheets	*58*
Practical Premise:	*61*
Chapter Eight: Identity	65
Face And Replace: Quality Word Lists	*72*
Change It	*78*
Practical Identity:	*79*
Chapter Nine: Resistance	82
Whose Voice	*88*
Practical Resistance:	*98*
Chapter Ten: Reasoning	102
Practical Reasoning	*111*
Chapter Eleven: Practice	115
Quality Word Practice	*120*
Practical Practice	*132*
Chapter Twelve: Action	135
Practical Action	*143*
Chapter Thirteen: Recap	146
Author Note:	*149*

PREFACE

This system of Right Thinking is deceptively simple. Only seven steps. There is no need to go into lengthy explanations of each step. They are easy to understand.

The only thing difficult about the process is doing it.

Without telling you exactly what to do, which never works for anything, especially for something like this, my intent is to give you enough guidance to easily find your way through this process.

You are in charge during this process—you and your God. Trust that. Listen to your heart, try out the logic, and do the work. The results will speak for themselves.

Chapter One: Preparing

Trust is the first step to love. —Premchand

Before you begin, there are a few things I would like you to know.

Please treat this book as a workbook for life. You can apply this Right Thinking system to any situation.

I would say to heal it, but really it produces a shift in thinking and that shift reveals what is actually going on, which results in what appears as healing.

This could be an emotional, physical, or mental healing because all healing begins the same way. By thinking rightly, which leads to the right action to take.

There is always action required. We have to participate. What that participation looks like depends on you and the situation.

But by applying Right Thinking, it will much more likely result in the right action.

Yes, Right Action is one of the seven steps, and we'll talk about it more when we get there, but in the meantime, it's essential to know that action will be required of us.

And since this book is about Right Thinking, it's clear that if we stick with what is Right, it will be the Right Action.

Because I have structured this book as a system, this book works well within a mastermind group or with a friend or two.

A like-minded community will help keep you on track, and as in all communities that support and listen to each other, it will magnify and hasten the results.

So see if you can find someone, or a group of people, to do this Right Thinking system with. Choose people that have your best interest in mind. I mean that last part. Be sure they have your best interest in mind.

Even the best family member or friend does not always have that intent. Choose carefully.

Find people who have the same desires as you to shift their lives and who you can trust to keep your "secrets."

Don't think you know anyone like this? Don't worry!

Read and follow this system on your own. I know that someday you will find people like that because like-minded, like-souled people find each other when the time is right.

If you need help, let me know. There might be a group going on that you can join, or I could be teaching a live class just as you begin this. You can find me at becalewis.com.

Take this time for deep thinking and the chance to rejuvenate your life. Don't wait. Get started.

Things will shift to bring you what you need and want if you are faithful to the practice and yourself. It always starts there.

With yourself. And faith.

Not sure you have it? You do. Or you wouldn't have opened this book.

That's enough faith right there.

****

He who believes himself to be far advanced in the spiritual life has not even made a good beginning. — Jean Pierre Camus

I remember the day I first taught this Right Thinking system. I had been playing with the concepts and steps on my own for a few years, and I was excited to see what others thought about it.

In my mind's eye, I can see the room that I rented in a tiny motel near Carlsbad beach in Southern California in 2003.

A small group of men and women joined me. We were off in the corner of a dark room, but none of us noticed. We were in the middle of applying something that could shift our thinking from what wasn't working to what would work.

Everyone in the room already knew me, and most of them were very familiar with The Shift System that I had been teaching for many years.

So I didn't have to explain the background of what we were doing. I just had to explain the Right Thinking steps to them.

We spent the day experiencing the shift of perception that the awareness of Truth brings. We rejoiced, knowing that we had taken the right steps towards healing.

And that's what we are doing together here—in a book instead of a class.

We are walking our thinking through *Seven Steps of Right Thinking* that will shift us out of our limited human belief systems and into the infinite possibilities of big T Truth and big R Reality.

Now, as then, as we keep our thought process within big T Truth, it results in an improved situation, whether it is a mental, physical, or an emotional problem.

Yes, these steps can be applied in any order, depending on the circumstances. But I have my favorite order, which is what we'll be doing in this book.

Often the work we do will affect areas we didn't expect to get better.

Why? Because everything is connected. And as we willingly shift our perceptions to a higher understanding of Truth, it affects everything in our world.

Shifting to big T Truth, we replace a false belief and perception that has hidden the Divine's perfection from us. And that produces what looks like healing.

However, beliefs and perceptions are stubborn, often persistent. Accepted as normal. But when we stop thinking of problems as something we have to fix, and instead as only a perception we have to shift, it becomes easier.

Before we begin, it's essential to understand that just because it is a belief or a perception doesn't mean it's not being experienced.

We are not discounting the experience of a belief while we shift it. That would be cruel and unkind.

Beliefs and perceptions are real to the person experiencing them, including ourselves.

Compassion, kindness, and practical help are essential components of Right Thinking.

And just because we call it a belief is not a reason to say to ourselves, or someone else, that we caused it because of our flawed thinking, or mistaken beliefs, or misperceptions. No.

Problems are never, ever, ever something we made happen. We, and they, are not to blame. No, sir. Never. Our choices may have kept us in a problem or put us there, but we didn't create them. We just took a road to where we didn't mean to go.

As soon as we fall into blame-thinking, we are back into the problem for ourselves or others.

Actually, we have made it worse because we have accepted it as reality. Then guilt and judgment are in charge because it would have us believe that we are God and can cause or create something.

Do you know what is really happening? We are misperceiving the Creation that the Divine Intelligence that is Love has put into place.

No. I don't know why. And I try not to care because as soon as I go there, whoops. There I am again, back into the belief of a problem.

Where I want to be is in the Mind of Love. I

want to see the world the way Infinite Intelligence sees it. Experience it the way omnipresent Love experiences it.

When we achieve that state of being—bam—what appears as a problem dissolves.

Is it this immediate? Sometimes.

If we get that glimpse of the Truth that these seven steps reveal and hold on to it, that problem has nowhere to exist.

But often, it is working through the so-called problem that gets us somewhere.

We have to recalibrate our perceptions and our beliefs. Realign ourselves with Truth repeatedly. Argue for Truth like a lawyer.

And since this is the way healing often happens, we might as well get every teeny bit of goodness out of the time it takes.

Like Jacob wrestling with the Angel, we can say, "Let me learn this lesson. I want wisdom. I want my eyes fully open to Truth."

Since that first class, I have taught the *Seven Steps To Right Thinking* course many times. Each time I learn more about how it works and better ways to present it.

The result? It's finally ready to be a book. This

book. Only seven steps. Use them any way that works for you.

When it's a class, it's seven weeks. If it is you at home, it's seven seconds, seven minutes, seven hours, seven days. Whatever it takes.

Systems are only guidelines. Not rules.

Let your intuition, the quiet voice within, guide you. You can't go wrong. I mean it. You can't go wrong.

You and I are the action, the expression of Divine Love.

And Love is never wrong!

Remember, problems are only a misperception. And we can shift that.

One more thing.

Because I think of this book as a course, I am writing it as if I am speaking to you in a class. I am thinking of you—yes, you—as I write.

You and I are One. That's the Truth. Now let's practice that Truth together using these seven steps and watch the world shift for the better. Not just for us, but for everyone.

I'll see you on the other side.

Chapter Two: Perception

There are things known and there are things unknown, and in between are the doors of perception.
—Aldous Huxley

There is no getting around it. Perception is reality. Perception creates reality. That means to get anything done or live a life of meaning and purpose, we have to continually shift our perceptions.

If you have read any of my other books, you have run across this idea before, but it bears repeating because it is easy to forget.

We are never trying to make something happen or stop something from happening.

What we are always doing is practicing, working on, shifting our perceptions towards the Infinite.

From there, everything falls into place.

But first, we have to be willing.

And then, if we are smart, and of course we are, we choose a point of view perception of the highest, best, most perfect life possible, and then we shift our state of mind perception to match.

Why not? No one wants to live in fear, or poverty, or ill health, or unhappiness.

However, we have all experienced someone who refuses to see a solution because their point of view perception or paradigm does not include that solution.

We've heard the excuses. "People are not meant to fly. No one can run a four-minute mile. Go to the moon? Impossible."

Usually, our shifts aren't this huge. But every shift of perception, every moment of willingness to admit that something better is possible, changes our lives.

Yes, every change in perception, from trying a new brand of a product to letting go of how we used to do something and trying a different way, shifts our experience.

However, it doesn't do any good to choose a new perception that only includes a new point of view. We have to align our entire belief system with it. I call this the state of mind perception.

Our point of view and state of mind perceptions must be in harmony with each other. Otherwise, it's a push-pull process that keeps us stuck in the problem.

Shifting our point of view perception is what the *Bible* might call the letter of the law. Good to have, but it's not what brings healing. It's the spirit of the law that does, and our state of mind perception is just that.

Not putting the two together is like calling ourselves a good person and then harming another on purpose—something we see all too often in the world.

Religious wars are a misalignment between point of view and state of mind perceptions.

Thinking others must conform to our perspective because it is what God wants of us, by hating and destroying those that don't believe as we do, is often the result.

That is not Right Thinking, and is what we want to rewrite for ourselves.

For example, we could have the point of view that the Divine supplies all our needs, but wake up each morning in fear of not having enough.

That is a misalignment between our point of view and state of mind, and that misalignment will not allow us to experience the healing that we desire.

Emotion, or state of mind, overrides our point of view.

Advertisers know this. That's why they use techniques to bring our feelings, wants, and desires into alignment with what they want us to believe—that their product is the best one available, and we need it.

Using this Right Thinking system, it becomes easier and easier to not agree with anything that isn't for the highest good, not only for ourselves but also for others.

First, we need to choose the highest point of view that we can imagine.

Here is the point of view I am using throughout this book.

- *Perfection is already present. Everywhere. There is only one creation, and it is Spiritual. It is the universe in which we live.*

Yes. I know. It doesn't feel like this most of the time. That's okay. It's still Truth.

- *The Divine is the intelligent omnipresence of Love and is the one and only creator. Not the creator of our material perception. It is the creator, designer, infinite intelligence of Spiritual Reality.*

Sounds good, right? It is. I love it. I believe it. It is, with no equivocation, my point of view.

I choose this point of view because I know that what I perceive to be reality magnifies, and I want, need, and desire to live a life filled with purpose, love, creativity, plenty, etc.

Yes, I have to remind myself of this point of view all the time. It takes practice since it is not the worldview.

Now comes the next part.

We want to move our state of mind into alignment with this point of view, and we need tools to do this. We need ways we can get better at the practice.

Right Thinking is one of those ways.

If we can bring our point of view and state of mind into complete alignment with the Truth of everyone's perfection as the idea, expression, reflection, of the Divine Principle of all Life, then the illusion of a problem falls away, and we experience what is called healing.

Sometimes that happens in a moment, and sometimes the problem takes time to fade away.

Sometimes we will be so engrossed in Truth we'll forget that we had a problem. Because even though healing is the expected result, our desire lies in understanding more about our true Spiritual nature as the reflection of the Divine.

Practicing this point of view means we have to give up how we—within the belief that we are human—think it should be.

This is because we could never, in our wildest dreams, come up with a better outcome than what letting go of our ego will reveal.

Before we start, let me take a moment and say how grateful I am for you.

Everyone who chooses a path of Right Thinking, the spiritual path, is a light for everyone else. As you shift your perception, it helps the entire world move into the harmony of Divine Love.

You have chosen the path of a spiritual warrior, a singer of harmony, a dancer of Spirit. Thank you.

Chapter Three: Your Way

> *To live content with small means; to seek elegance rather than luxury, and refinement rather than fashion; to be worthy, not respectable, and wealthy, not rich; to listen to stars and birds, babes and sages, with open heart; to study hard; to think quietly, act frankly, talk gently, await occasions, hurry never; in a word, to let the spiritual, unbidden and unconscious, grow up through the common—this is my symphony.* —William Henry Channing

Are you ready to begin? You can decide now how long you want to take to go through this book. Take one step a day, or one step a week, or one step an hour.

Do what works for you. However you decide, it will be perfect for you. If it's not, make adjustments until it is.

A few years ago, I thought I would emulate some of my author friends and write a book every six weeks. Yes, some of them were doing it even faster than that, but with everything else I was doing, I knew six weeks was my limit.

I lasted through three books.

And then I discovered that writing that quickly wasn't satisfying for me. At all. I felt rushed continuously and always worried and anxious.

For what? I asked myself. To be like someone else? To make more money?

I knew that if those were the reasons, it would never work. I would eventually sabotage myself to make it stop. This is not a good way to live.

Through the next few books, I kept fiddling with the process until I discovered my timing.

And yes, I still have to remind myself to keep writing when it gets too hard. But that's true for anything, even if it is something we love to do.

It was the rhythm of it I was after. What could I do that kept me motivated but not overwhelmed?

Do this system of Right Thinking the same way. Stay motivated. But don't make yourself crazy, trying to keep a schedule that isn't yours.

One way to figure out what works for you is to ask yourself if what you are doing is sustainable. Can you keep it up?

That's what I did with writing. I changed to a schedule sustainable for me. I keep adjusting the schedule so I can keep doing this without making myself so overwhelmed that I have to fight the desire to quit.

Not to get overwhelmed is a good intent for me. Ask my husband. He can tell when I have made myself crazy by making myself a list that no one can keep up with for long.

Of course, he doesn't like it when I am reacting to being overwhelmed because he has to work around it. I know you know what I mean.

When we are not paying attention to what works for us, not only do we make life hard for ourselves but also for those around us.

No one should become stuck in the status quo. But don't give yourself so much to do that it becomes debilitating. Life is not static. We can, and continuously must, keep adjusting what we do to fit the changing dynamics of daily life.

Do this system. Practice it. But do it your way.

In the process, don't harm yourself or anyone else. Always aim for the next right step. You can tell if it's the next step because it will bring more joy for anyone your life touches—starting with your own.

Alright. Now that you have chosen a schedule that you think will work for you, knowing that you can change it, we will spend some time together doing the most important thing we can do—shift our everyday habitual thinking to Right Thinking.

Right Thinking is the thinking which begins and ends with the desire to raise our understanding of the Infinite, and experience the results in our lives and the lives of those around us, both near and far.

We begin with the first step of Right Intent.

Where else would we start? We have to begin with Right Intent in order for everything else to begin with the correct Principle.

We start with our desire to choose a clear intent for every thought and action. To ground it in the first commandment of "Thou shalt have no other Gods before me."

Years ago, I discovered a prayer that helps me establish my intent in every action, but especially in the ones I am afraid to do or don't want to do, which—not surprisingly—are often the same thing.

It is part of a poem written by Mary Baker Eddy, and it goes like this, "... my prayer, some daily good to do for Thine, for Thee; and offering pure of Love whereto God leadeth me."

What a great place to start!

To make things easy, I'll assume you are doing this system one step at a time for a week. Doing it this way, the first time through this, will give us time to absorb each step's meaning and practice it.

For this first week, let's be sure we are thinking and acting from Right Intent.

To do this, we must pull in all our perception skills. Don't worry. We will have lots of practice.

As you do this course, pause often, observe without judgment, and listen deeply.

Here we go!

Chapter Four: Begin

The most difficult thing is the decision to act, the rest is merely tenacity. The fears are paper tigers. You can do anything you decide to do. You can act to change and control your life; and the procedure, the process is its own reward. —Amelia Earhart

No matter what we do, it is always best to start with our Right Intent.

Many people start with a goal or a to-do list, but not us. We always begin with intent. We will get to goals and to-dos later.

But why do we start with intent?

Because our goals can change, and if our goals change, then so do the to-dos for reaching those goals. That is a good thing because it means we are adjusting to changing circumstances.

But intents stay the same. We may change our intent to a different one, but once we have an intent, then the goals and to-dos will naturally fall into place.

Another way to see the difference is that intent is not measurable, although you will see and feel the difference. Goals and to-do lists are.

For example, as a writer, I intend to communicate clearly, entertain, and shift thinking to infinite possibilities.

How many books, what kind of books, when to publish them, how to write them, and how to sell more books, fall into goals, and to-do lists, and are things that I can measure. They grew out of my intent.

Remember, actions are measurable, intents are not. Remembering that will help us decide if what we want is a goal or an intent.

We must always, always begin with intent.

Not only will we be more focused, but with clear intent, we will be more content with whatever we choose to do.

Think of your intent as the why behind the action,

For example, to write this book or teach the class, I had to set an intent. You might say that I had a goal to teach a class. Sure. But why? Because without that why, I could easily lose interest or get pulled off track.

So first, what was my intent for putting together this Seven Steps for Right Thinking?

I wanted to have a path to walk for when I, or anyone else, needed to experience healing.

It's the "anyone else" that I always want to be present in my intents. I want my intents to align with what I have accepted as a mission: share ways to shift thinking and lives towards the Infinite.

Yes, I could have said this was my goal, but since it is the reason, or the why behind the action and is not measurable, I recognize this as my intent.

However, although intent—or the why—is always powerful, we are interested in Right Intent.

Someone who has lost their moral compass could set an intent to do harm.

That is never our intent.

So let's review what we mean by Right.

****

Look for strengths in people, not weaknesses; for good, not evil. Most of us find what we search for. —J. Wilbur Chapman

All the words that we will use in this system are familiar: intent, premise, reasoning, practice, action, etc. We use these words and do these actions all the time. What makes this system work is that we put the word Right in front of them.

When the word Right is an adjective, it includes the words justified and acceptable.

Do we want to use the words justified and acceptable in our definition? Usually not. At least we have to see them as warning signs to look deeper.

If we have to justify our decisions, intent, and actions, we may be heading down the wrong path.

Justification is a warning sign to ourselves that we are probably not making the right choice. We are making a more comfortable choice, a more familiar choice. When we do that, we have to look again to make sure it is the right choice.

And is doing only partially the right thing acceptable? Usually not. And yes, sometimes we have to make concessions and compromises. But even then we need to base them on the Right Intent.

Which brings me back to religious wars, well, actually any war. Wars have to be justified by the ones declaring them. They need to make their actions acceptable to themselves first so they can convince others.

On a smaller scale, we may justify why we cheat, look away when someone needs our help, or gossip instead of help.

This doesn't mean that sometimes we have to justify our actions when we need to do something that others might consider wrong.

Is it wrong to steal bread when you are hungry?

Or was it more wrong to allow situations where someone is hungry and then punishing them for doing their best to survive?

We know the answer.

We always have to see actions from a higher Intent, and it is the highest right we currently know and considering the circumstances.

But if that still small voice says that it isn't the right thing to do based on the law of Love, it's best to stop and reexamine the motive behind the intent.

As a noun, the word Right means that which is morally correct, just, or honorable.

And that's what we mean by it, too. But that brings us back to questioning what is morally correct, just, and honorable.

I think we know it when we see it. Or understand it when we feel it. It's right when it doesn't break Spiritual laws or the spirit of another being.

We will discover more about what is morally correct, just, or honorable to us during this practice.

And why does it matter?

There are three principal reasons.

First, because when we don't choose the morally good, correct path, everything eventually falls apart.

And second, because we intend to be good people. How do I know that is one of your intents? Because you wouldn't be reading this book if you didn't want that for yourself.

And the third reason is that we know that *what we perceive to be reality magnifies.*

That means that if we believe and act as if it's true—that good is the only power—then good we get. When we give morally ambiguous choices the power, that's what we get.

Which brings me back to the first reason for choosing the highest Intent we know in each moment.

If we don't, eventually, everything falls apart.

While I was writing this book, the world was in the middle of the 2020 pandemic. For the first time in recorded history, everyone in the world stopped doing what they were doing.

COVID 19 literally stopped the world. It gave us all both a microscope and a wide-angle view of human nature and people's choices. It gave us a chance to reset everything.

We discovered that some people, perhaps unconsciously, wanted to express their personal freedom more than they cared about possibly hurting others. That's not a Right Intent.

It was "I have a right to do this" point of view and involved justification and rationalization.

When we make these kinds of choices, we may overlook the broader interpretations of what our actions mean and their consequences.

Everyone made hard decisions. But only the solutions made with the safety of everyone as a community in mind could be called Right Intent.

We discovered that most people are kind, caring, and thoughtful. Most people go out of their way to help. We also found that it was easy to be caught up in fear. To lash out and call it a right of freedom.

Everyone had to rethink their lives and make choices about what to do next. The decisions and choices made from our highest understanding at the time of the right thing to do were Right Intent.

In this book, that is what we will practice doing.

The more we practice, the better we will be at it. We'll change our intents as we gain wisdom, which will indeed happen.

Remember, the intent is an overall decision. It's why we do things. It is not a goal. It is not a list of to-dos.

As we set our intents, we'll do our best to select morally good, just, kind, and expansive ones.

However, as we gain insight and wisdom, we will also expand our awareness of what we are doing and have a clearer understanding of if it is right.

That is a good thing. An intent to move into a higher understanding of our true spiritual nature underlies everything about The Shift System and Right Thinking.

Narrowing it down, so we don't have so many words to say, we use the word Right.

So now that we know what we mean by Right, let's get started with setting Right Intents, and that begins with ourselves.

Chapter Five: You First

When you move, the Universe moves. When you reach, it reaches. When you stretch, it stretches. But always, you must go first. —Mike Dooley

I mentioned that my intent behind putting together this Seven Step System for Right Thinking was because I wanted to have a path to walk when I—or anyone else—needed to experience healing.

Notice how my intent starts with me and then reaches out to others.

I point this out because I want you to start with yourself too. Not stay with yourself, start with yourself.

Too many of us were trained to accept that we must think of others first. But doing it that way does not work in the long run, because it's not sustainable.

The commandment to do unto others as we would have them do unto us means that we better be taking good care of ourselves first because that is the only way we can continue to do good unto others.

Sure, some people don't need to be reminded to think about themselves first. These are the people who don't care how their actions affect others. I doubt if they are reading this book.

But we all know them. And if you are part of one of these people's lives, the likelihood that you suffer because of them is high.

Because without the desire to assist others, those people are dangerous to themselves and the world.

Right Intent must be an intent that does no harm and blesses everyone it touches.

Too many people get lost in the desire for power and lose their awareness of their connection to Divine essence and their obligation to care for others as themselves.

Can this system be applied to healing a person or situation harmful to you personally or the world? Absolutely.

However, it will be your perception of them that heals. We are not in charge of what that will look like. However, we know it will be better for you and them—if they are willing.

The underlying and motivating intent behind Right Thinking is spiritual renovation.

To give you an example of what Right Intent could look like, this is the one I made for the class and for this book:

- To practice clean, clear thinking, which will, in turn, dissolve the darkness of fear and ignorance.

- To renew hopes and aspirations within ourselves and share it with others.

- To pour out a cleansing flood of spiritual Right Thinking for ourselves, our families, the world.

- To rejoice together, knowing that the reign of harmony is already within us, and present for everyone, everywhere.

Within the class, we added this intent:

- To fully participate in this community of like-minded souls so that every member feels the support and encouragement of walking with a group of people on the same path with everyone's best interests in mind.

To make this book as practical as possible, because spirituality is useless if it's not practical, I made up a person, I've named her Sally, and I will walk you through how she might apply this system to her problem(s).

But first, let's look at some examples of what people who took the class stated as their intent.

Then we'll move on to Sally's and yours.

Sample Right Intents:

To live, hear, and share Truth.
To live in this world as Joy and Grace
To exude Enthusiasm.
To be grateful for God's blessings.
To listen carefully.
To be productive.
To express joy each day.
To use technology to further my life's purpose.
To know I can share my gifts.
To notice where my attention has been going.
To block all negative influences from my life.
To accept and recognize joy around me.
To feel the divine energy of Spirit.
To stay in the Now.
Wherever God leads me, I shall go.
To find focus.
To dance for exercise & meditate for relaxation.
To reconnect to my inner plug.
To transform myself and my life.
To get more organized.
To stay present.
To be grateful and reset everything that matters.
To put my foot down and say no to error.
To focus on love, not fear.
To make a daily productive schedule.
To embrace my "new normal."
To celebrate going within.
To develop a life full of happy, healthy choices.
To grow deep roots.
To keep in touch with family and friends.

You can see that these intents cover a wide range of desires for what they wanted to get out of the class.

So let's begin with you. Take a moment and ask yourself, "what is my intent for reading this book and learning this system?"

So as not to get overwhelmed and to be sustainable, pick just one for now.

This system is not going anywhere. Once you get familiar with it, you can run through it in a flash as many times a day as you desire.

For now, you'll pick just one overall intent for the practice.

But first, let's meet Sally.

Sally

Our fictional friend Sally may feel familiar. That won't be surprising.

We all have the same kinds of issues or problems or situations to work through at different times in our lives.

If not us, someone we know and love may have experienced them.

Hopefully, Sally's walk through this system of thoughtful thinking will be helpful for your practice.

Okay. Story time.

Sally has more than one problem on her mind and has trouble deciding which one to focus on first.

She doesn't feel all that healthy. She's gained weight over the years and doesn't have consistent exercise habits. In general, she hasn't been feeling well for years, and now she is worried that she might have something seriously wrong with her.

Her children often test her patience. She wishes she could do more for them, while not interfering with their ability to find their own happiness.

Work. Well, it could be better. She feels underappreciated and underpaid. Besides, people act in ways that upset her at work, and she often brings that upset home. Sally is tempted to quit her job and do something that brings her more joy, but what?

Besides, she and her husband need to make sure they make enough money for their future. And the world seems to be going crazy now, so who can trust anything?

And even if she knew what she wanted to do, she can't choose to change her life right now. Her mother is getting older and will need more care. Who will do it if not her?

Her husband isn't much help.

He has become increasingly fearful. It's hard for her to admit that he is spending money on things that help him escape. And he takes out his anger and fear on her. Sometimes he scares her. Mostly he annoys her.

Sally has things going on, doesn't she?

There are many things she can choose from for this first pass through this system.

She takes a few days, but finally, Sally decides on her overall Intent.

Here's what Sally decided.

- Overall Intent: *Get my health back.*

Chapter Six: Intent

> *We are social creatures to the inmost centre of our being. The notion that one can begin anything at all from scratch, free from the past, or unindebted to others, could not conceivably be more wrong.* —Karl Popper

We need to add a few steps to this Right Thinking process before going any further.

It would be lovely if by merely choosing our intent, everything would fall into place with no more effort on our part.

But you and I know it doesn't work that way. Too many old beliefs and habits get in the way. So we need to address this problem. We need to root out those old perceptions and replace them with ones that will let us experience the Right Intents that we are setting.

Remember the point of view and state of mind modes of perception that we talked about in Chapter Two?

They are the key to making these shifts, so I have some thinking exercises for you to do for both these modes.

Don't pass these exercises by thinking they aren't necessary. They are.

First, an explanation or two, and then I'll use Sally as an example of how they work.

Because what we don't know does hurt us, we need to discover what hidden perceptions have been driving our lives around without our conscious consent.

Although sometimes we are aware of these perceptions, beliefs, and habits, we usually ignore them, either because we don't think they are doing us any harm or changing them seems too difficult.

Sometimes we don't change them because we don't think it is allowed, or shifting them will take us into uncharted territory.

Yes, we have the Divine's permission to change our beliefs, because otherwise, how will we move to a higher understanding of Love?

And yes, we will move into uncharted—for us—territory. But help is always waiting for us.

And it shall come to pass, that before they call, I will answer; and while they are yet speaking, I will hear. —Isaiah 65:24

Yes, life will change. That's the point, after all. But it will change for the better.

Shifting Our Point of View

Much of what goes on in our lives begins with the point of view we have accepted about ourselves.

Happily, we have a choice about how much of it we want to keep. We can change it. We don't have to accept anything about ourselves if it doesn't align with our true spiritual natures.

None of us has escaped this problem. So as we work on Right Thinking, let's discover what is not right thinking.

Although we will address what is Right Identity as one of the seven steps, we first have to uncover those perceptions, beliefs, and habits that we have accepted as accurate about who we are.

Start a **written** list of what you say to yourself about who you are. Include what others tell you about who you are, and what the worldview says you are.

This list is essential to uncovering the beliefs that underlay everything we believe about ourselves. If you had a mouse in your house, would you search it out before it did damage? What about a raccoon? Or a moose?

Hidden thoughts and beliefs are the same. They do damage to our lives. Root them out. To get started, all you have to do is write them down. It's an observation practice.

Some are good things to identify with, others not so much. It doesn't matter, add them all to the list. Keep writing.

The most important thing of all—besides noticing—is not judging. Just notice. Give this exercise your physical attention, but not your emotional attention.

This exercise will continue all our lives. It's part of re-writing our story. Don't worry. I'll remind you to do it.

SHIFTING OUR STATE OF MIND

But what about our state of mind?

In our world, there are so many things going on that affect how we feel that it's imperative to pay attention to our state of mind.

There are many techniques to calming the mind and bringing us back to the harmony that underlies all of Life.

We could meditate. Go for a walk. Sit in nature. Listen to bird songs. Breathe.

Our intent is to quiet the mind and the thoughts that tell us we are not doing it right.

Some people call this the inner critic, the judge, the monkey mind.

It always lies.

Let's see how all this works with Sally.

SALLY'S INTENT STORY:

Just writing her desire to get her health back as the overall intent for this practice made Sally feel better. She was going to do it. Finally.

Sally figures that she will have the energy to deal with the other problems in her life if she begins with how she feels about her health.

She had been putting off dealing with her health for far too long. Each year that has gone by has not made her body feel better. Now all she wants is to wake up in the morning and not be upset about what she sees in the mirror. She wanted to be able to walk to the mailbox without something hurting.

Maybe she could never feel or look like she did at eighteen, but she would try. How could it hurt?

Sally laughed when she said that to herself. It might hurt. Because getting her health back meant she would have to find out why she had let herself get to this point.

That was what she needed to find out first. Sally grabbed some sheets of paper and stuck them around the house, ready to write down what she believed about herself and her health habits.

Sally realized she didn't really want to do find out what she believed and had accepted as truth. It was work. And hearing all those beliefs in her head was probably going to make her feel worse.

But she did want to get her health back and feel better, so she just wrote them down anyway and tried not to judge herself.

Some thoughts were in her own voice, others were things she had heard her parents say, and some of it was what she assumed was a worldview, like genetics.

After a few days, Sally noticed that there weren't as many thoughts as she imagined there would be. Most of them were simply a variation on a theme that she was a failure and a loser.

However, Sally made careful notes about the details of why she was letting herself be called a failure and a loser.

Sally figured that they were ideas she would be re-writing as she practiced Right Thinking.

It was hard to keep from being upset with what she was hearing, but Sally knew that wouldn't solve anything, and she was ready to let go of the past and move on. To help her point of view, Sally sat outside every day for a few minutes and watched the clouds go by. She started listening to a meditation tape during her lunch break. Five minutes made a big difference.

By the end of the week, the list was long but less threatening. Now that she was noticing what was driving her thoughts, she felt better. Sally always knew something was going on without her knowledge, and now that she was looking right at it, she felt more in control.

The intent to feel better and get her health back seemed possible. Sometimes, for a few minutes a day, it even felt real. That made it easy to write out her Right Intent.

Here's what Sally decided.

Overall Right Intent: *Get my health back.*
Right Intent: *To feel better.*

Your Right Intent

I arise in the morning torn between a desire to improve the world and a desire to enjoy the world. This makes it hard to plan the day. —E. B. White

Since we are intentionally setting intents, we get to be very clear about what we are choosing.

I used to call this first step, Right Desire. So if you substitute the word desire for intent, it might be easier. What is it that you want? What is it that you desire?

These intents, while remaining morally correct (which means by you choosing it, others will eventually benefit, and no commandments are broken) are all about you.

All of this work is all about you.

This is a Right Intent. Because when we get ourselves straight, the world around us straightens out with us.

Instead of starting from the outside, we begin from the inside.

So, what do you desire? Feel the answer. Spend time with it. Does it bring you joy? Remember, emotion will drive the outcome.

It's okay that thinking about this brings fear or worry. Stretching out of comfort zones can do that.

But when fear or worry set the intent, we will never get to what we desire, and we, and the world, will not benefit.

However, if fear and worry follow the intent, or try to stop you from choosing it, you just might be on the right track.

Being emotionally comfortable is never the intent. We aim for spiritual growth, wisdom, understanding, possibilities, and expansion, which often feels uncomfortable.

However, it will be worth it. And don't worry. We'll deal with the fear and worry later.

Just move forward, take a deep breath, and set your Right Intent. And as always, as you gain wisdom and understanding, you can change it.

Change is good. And since change is always going on, that is the premise we are going to adopt.

Practical Intent

I am writing this book as a weekly practice, but you can choose the time frame that works for you.

However, doing it as a weekly practice at least the first time around gives you time to pay attention to your thinking and the outcomes.

Remember that these intents are meant for you. They have to be right for you. Be careful to not choose an intent that someone else said is correct, or gave to you, or you grew up with, or that's how it has always been, or it will gain you points, or what everyone else is doing.

These assignments for each step of Right Thinking will help ground the system, repair old beliefs, build habits that work for you, dissolve untruths about yourself and others, and reveal your true self to yourself.

STEP ONE: RIGHT INTENT

My overall intent for reading this book:

My Right Intent:

• Begin a list as to how you find yourself identifying yourself. Notice what you say to yourself. Notice what others say about you. Write it down! Note which ones are always being said. We will do this for a few weeks. Listen. Don't judge. Just keep notes.

• Choose at least one way that you will calm your thinking, quiet the mind and bring it into harmony with your intent. Perhaps meditation of some kind. Walking by yourself. Sitting in nature. Listening to bird songs.

INTENT REVIEW

Before we head into the next week's Right Thinking step, take a moment and review what happened in the past week.

Maybe this seems like a step you could skip, but please don't. Remember, it's what we don't notice that drives our lives without our consciously choosing it.

Reviewing the week helps ground the work into something tangible, and although our intents are not measurable, progress is. Even if the progress doesn't feel good, note that too. Everything is relevant for shifting our perceptions.

Things I noticed:

Ways I am stuck:

Things that have changed:

Chapter Seven: Premise

And God saw every thing that he had made, and, behold, it was very good. —Genesis 1:31

Old premises and perceptions that keep us stuck are habits. We are going to shift them.

Our neighbor across the street always backs out into the road. It makes both Del and me crazy. He has a turnaround in his driveway, so it would be easy to come into the street in a way that isn't a hazard to himself and others. Why is he backing out when he doesn't have to?

Is it a habit, or is he not paying attention, or is he only thinking of himself? Or all three?

As we pay more attention to our habits and preconceived ideas, better ways of doing things will pop up in our thinking. We'll want to smack our foreheads and ask ourselves why we didn't see that before.

Because habits and unconscious choices act as blinders, we only see what we expect to see. As we shift our perceptions to a more expansive view, many things we never saw before appear before us.

Using the practice of Right Thinking we will search for, and root out of ourselves, habitual thinking. As we do so, more and more evidence of infinite possibilities will become evident.

Last week, we set a Right Intent, and now we are moving to Right Premise.

But what is a premise?

Let's start again with the dictionary definition. As a noun, the word premise contains a logic that goes like this: If the premise is true, then the conclusion must be true.

Or it's a proposition which forms the basis of a theory. As a verb, it works as a base for a theory.

Both definitions work with what we are going to do with our premise.

However, to get to the Right part of it, we need to do a quick review of how the two modes of perception—point of view and state of mind—work because they form a premise.

We know that what we perceive to be reality magnifies, which means we get more of what we believe to be true. Some people call this a self-fulfilling prophecy. Either way, it's how human life works.

Our human brains filter out anything that doesn't match what we believe or want to know. It's probably for the best because there is no way we can take in all that is going on around us.

However, since you are reading this book, I will assume that you have a sense that something, we can call it God, or infinite Mind, or the Great Mystery, or the Divine, exists, and we are Its creation.

Even though our human senses can't sense this, or no one can "prove" it, we know that it's true.

And we yearn to know more of this Truth and have our lives more closely match this Infinite One, which has to be harmonious and Good.

I argue why this is true in all the books in *The Shift Series*, so for now, let's agree on this: There is an Infinite Intelligent One that is omnipresent Love. Good exists and is the only power.

We are choosing this point of view because it's true. And even though we don't fully understand how it could be true, it is what we want to experience.

We want to experience Intelligent omnipresent Love. We want to rest in the knowledge that Good is the only power. We want to experience a life that results from that point of view.

So we've done it. We've chosen our point of view. It is also the basis for everything that follows from here, starting with Right Premise.

A reminder. Yes, the more we hold to this point of view, the more we should experience the ultimate harmony that this point of view promises.

And we will. Except.

If our state of mind does not accept this point of view as a valid premise, instead we let worry, guilt, self-pity, or fear take over, those emotions will control how much we experience it.

Of course, all these emotions exist for all of us and will probably coexist with us until we break the bonds of a human perspective. But they don't have to be in charge.

Whatever moves us into the state of mind where we can hear and experience the harmony of the Life, that's what we need to do.

Because—and this is a huge because—we remember that if our state of mind is not in agreement with our point of view, it is our state of mind that will project more of what we experience.

At all times, we must fight to stay within a common point of view and state of mind that Good and harmony are in charge of this moment and every moment.

We always have the opportunity to reset ourselves to a better point of view and bring our state of mind into harmony with it.

That said, now we are ready to set our Right Premise for the Right Intent that we are focusing on this week.

It doesn't have to sound "spiritual." It just has to be set into a premise that begins with the point of view and state of mind that we wish to experience.

If we worry about whether we are right, it's not—right, that is. Because worry, guilt, fear, shame, and uncertainty are trying to set the premise.

We can change our premises as we learn more, even if it is only a minute from now.

In fact, we have to keep changing it, because there is no way that what we believe and know right now is absolutely correct.

We can't expect that we know everything in this moment any more than a baby knows what it will know after fifty years of experience.

But we can keep stepping forward.

Before we set our Right Premise, let's look at how Sally is choosing hers.

Sally's Premise

It's been an interesting week for Sally. There were days she forgot to pay attention to her Overall Intent to get her health back and her Right Intent to feel better. When she remembered, she was often doing the exact opposite thing she intended to do.

Sally thought that setting the intent to get her health back and feel better would motivate her to eat better, maybe exercise a little every day, but that only happened the first day. After that, it was a struggle.

Instead, it felt as if everything worked against her. Her husband didn't like the meal she cooked. She stubbed her toe, so it was hard to walk, and in general, she felt terrible.

Sally was tempted to stop doing this Right Thinking practice if it was going to make things worse, but she knew she was tired of how things were. Besides, she was always giving up on what she wanted for herself. This time she would stick it out because she really wanted to feel better.

Sally's list of things she said about herself had grown to stacks of little pieces of paper scattered around the house. When she read them over, she couldn't believe how often she told herself that she was a loser.

Sally knew she wasn't supposed to judge, but she felt like a loser, so it was hard not to agree with that voice in her head, making her feel even more like a loser.

She had to give herself a pep talk every morning. And when she started feeling sorry for herself, she had to write that down too, trying not to agree with, or judge, what seemed so true. She had made a mess of her life.

The one thing she managed to do almost every day was sit quietly on her back porch for a few minutes before she left for work. Sometimes she sat in the dark because she was getting up earlier. It was strange, but she liked it. She didn't know if that was meditation, but it felt good, and she planned to do more of that.

Sally was definitely ready to begin her second week of Right Thinking. She was ready for things to get better.

Figuring out the Right Premise to add to her Right Intent seemed strange. And difficult. She would have to say something that didn't feel true to her, especially after such a hard week.

But eventually, she came up with something she hoped would help. Sally decided that since she was supposed to state a Right Premise with the point of view that everything was already perfect and good, that meant that she must be feeling good despite all appearances to the contrary.

She loved that she didn't have to make something happen, she only had to let go and see what was already true, even if it seemed fanciful. However, it would be wonderful if it turned out to be true.

After thinking it through, Sally decided that

since she was the Divine's perfect reflection, she must reflect perfect health.

Did she believe it? Her rational mind did not, but Sally decided to trust the process. If what she believed to be true magnified, she would stop the habit of thinking of herself as a mess and start seeing herself as already healthy.

And, she vowed to herself, she would spend time actively shifting her state of mind into harmony with that perception which meant, she decided, more meditation time and perhaps a trip to the park to sit outside and listen to the birds.

It couldn't hurt, and it just might help, she told herself.

Here's where Sally is so far:

Overall Right Intent: *Get my health back.*
Right Intent: *To feel better.*
Right Premise: *I am already healthy and I feel great.*

FACE AND REPLACE: I CHOOSE SHEETS

The human mind is composed of chasms and sunless abysses, layer upon layer in which there are secret chambers where alien natures can hide undetected. — Thomas De Quincey

We have to do something with that list of perceptions we have been collecting about ourselves.

We are going to face them head-on. And then, replace those negative perceptions with what is true, using two perception shifting tools, I Choose sheets and Quality Words lists.

This week we will add the I Choose tool to face what we say to ourselves and replace it consciously.

Doing I Choose sheets will help bring our state of mind into harmony with our point of view, and we know how important that is!

Remember, it's our unconscious choices that are building our current life experience. We have been uncovering our unconscious hidden choices and perceptions and beginning to choose consciously.

In the early 1800s, Thomas De Quincey invented the term *unconscious*. He maintained that thoughts and emotions we don't know we have can control us.

Yes. Not that they can—they are. Therefore uncovering and eliminating hidden thoughts and emotions, or shifting the ones that don't serve us, is imperative.

Consciously choosing, we are aware of our thoughts and emotions. And standing in the premise we have chosen, we are moving away from our perception of ourselves as human and into our true spiritual nature.

Yes, consciously choosing looks like affirmations, but they are even more potent because instead of overlying a truth on top of something, we are cleaning out the mess first.

Let's use Sally to see what that would look like.

Sally keeps hearing that she is a loser. She says it to herself all the time.

First, she faces it.

On a sheet of paper, she writes:
"I am a loser."

Now she chooses to replace it.
I choose to see myself as a winner.

She listens and hears the monkey voice, inner critic, and judge say,
   "You've been a loser since the day you were born."

Sally's says,
"I choose to know that I am a child of God."

Monkey Voice
"You don't have a right to choose."

Sally:
"I choose to have a right."

Monkey Voice:

"Everything you do turns out wrong."

Sally:
"I choose that everything I do turns out for the best."

Monkey Voice:
"Your parents thought you were a loser, too."

Sally:
"I choose to see myself as a child of the One Father-Mother God."

Monkey Voice:
"There is no God."

Sally:
"I choose to know that there is One, and It doesn't create losers."

Okay, you get the idea. And yes, I Choose sheets could go on for pages and pages and veer off into multiple directions.

But always, always, Sally is going to consciously make her choices based on the best point of view that she can imagine.

Practical Premise:

Now it's your turn.

These assignments for each step of Right

Thinking will help ground the system, repair old beliefs, build habits that work for you, dissolve untruths about yourself and others, and reveal your true self to yourself.

These pages are designed to build on each other. First, Right Intent, then Right Premise.

You'll notice that I keep saying this week's. Why? Because if you wish, you could change your intent, etc., every week.

However, for the first time through this system, I suggest you stick with one. After you get the hang of it, feel free to change it up.

And yes, we keep writing them out. Writing things down over and over again helps override the programming that says otherwise.

Step Two: Right Premise

My overall intent for reading this book:

My Right Intent:

My Right Premise:

- Continue noticing how you are self identifying,

and how others see you.

- Start an I Choose sheet, and keep it going until that voice has nothing left to say.

- Choose at least one way that you will calm your thinking, quiet the mind and bring it into harmony with your intent. Do a meditation of some kind. Walking by yourself. Sitting in nature. Listening to bird songs.

Premise Review

Before we head into the next week's Right Thinking step, take a moment and review what happened in the past week.

Maybe this seems like a step you could skip, but please don't. Remember, it's what we don't notice that drives our lives without our consciously choosing it.

Reviewing the week helps ground the work into something tangible, and although our intents are not measurable, progress is. Even if the progress doesn't feel good, note that too. Everything is relevant for shifting our perceptions.

Things I noticed:

Ways I am stuck:

Things that have changed:

Chapter Eight: Identity

Know thyself. —Inscribed on The Temple of Apollo at Delphi

To know thyself is the beginning of wisdom.
—Socrates

Knowing others is intelligence, knowing yourself is true wisdom. —The Tao Te Ching

This above all, to thine own self be true.
—William Shakespeare

Right Identity is not our human identity. It's our identity as the expression of the Divine.

It's hard to see, let alone feel and know in our hearts and minds, our Divine identity, and then be faithful to it.

Since we live in what appears as a human identity, let's talk about that first, because it will give us clues to who we truly are.

As humans, we stand in front of a mirror and see a face and a body. Sometimes we like it. Most often we don't.

As time moves on, we see and feel the changes that the belief of time invokes. Once again, sometimes we like those changes. Most often, we don't.

However, our mirror is not the only way to see our human selves. We can also use profile tests, astrology, the Chinese Zodiac, etc. as mirrors. Sometimes we like what they tell us. Sometimes we don't.

However, in all cases, it's essential to pay attention to what the reflection is telling us because only then can we change our perception about ourselves, whether it is what we believe or what others believe about us.

Worldview is a powerful belief system. We need to look at that mirror because we won't consciously shift what we don't know is being claimed about who we are.

Looking in an actual mirror, we can determine how we want to appear to the outside world. We make sure our shirt is not on inside out, and our hair isn't sticking out at weird angles.

Profile tests, and other mirrors like them, help us in the same way. They show us things about ourselves.

Once again, it doesn't matter if we like those things or not.

Since all reflections only reveal to us what our human self or the worldview believes, liking it or not liking it isn't the issue.

Knowing about it gives us the power to shift it and become more aware of our pure spiritual essence.

These reflection instruments can reveal our unique gifts to us. Once we see them and accept them, then we can take those gifts and expand them.

Reflections also reveal our weaknesses so we can strengthen them. They provide "ah-ha" moments that can shift the way we live in the world.

As an example, when I learned that I'm an introvert, it shifted everything for me. I understood why I did things and how I had not set up my life to fit who I am.

At the time, I was a Certified Financial Planner. I loved the work, but not how I was doing it.

Realizing that as an introvert I "gassed up" by myself to spend my energy with people meant that the way my extroverted trainer—who "gassed up" by being with people—was teaching me to run my business, made me want to quit. Adjusting my days to match what I needed, I designed my business into one I loved.

Mirrors also reveal to us how other people perceive us.

Knowing this means we can adjust how we present ourselves to communicate more clearly based on what we are trying to accomplish. And since we are always responsible for how and what we communicate, this is essential information.

Other information these reflections convey can help us combat temptations that drag us away from or hide our true spiritual nature.

The mirror called the Enneagram does this exceptionally well. It not only reflects to us our true spiritual nature, but it also reveals unhealthy behavior so we can stop giving in to it or accepting it as accurate about ourselves.

We can see them as temptations and not realities.

And since much of our behavior is not something we notice, it's good to have any mirror that alerts us to it.

Even the best of friends will not tell us all about the irritating and ungodlike behavior that we may exhibit, and often are not aware that we are doing it.

Since we intend to discover and live as the Divine's expression, these are things we need to know.

Not knowing is not a strength; instead, it leaves us vulnerable.

There is another crucial reason for paying attention to what reflections reveal to us.

Anything that tells us something about our human expression, whether or not we believe it, the worldview does. Most of humankind does. And that hidden perception, energy, point of view—whatever we want to call it—does impact us.

If we don't know about it, we often do it and accept it as truth without consciously being aware that we are doing so.

When I learned that people believe that Tauruses don't like change, I made a conscious choice to not agree with that perception. I love change, new directions, and expansion.

And if I am being stubborn (after noticing that I am), I can ask myself if I am giving in to a belief about myself or being stubborn because I am not moving off of Truth.

If I don't feel like participating, is it because there is an untrue belief that an introvert stays silent, or because I am afraid to speak out and be present?

Reflections are not excuses to not do something we need to do or want to do. Nor are they traps or prisons. Most of all, we can not use them to justify limiting how we are expressing ourselves or treat others.

We don't give them power. We learn from them. And face and replace them as necessary.

The question always is: are we acting as the expression of the Divine? Or are we acting out of personality, ego, and beliefs about our human self?

None of us are alike—either humanly or Divinely.

Choosing our Right Identity, we become even more unique, not as a personality, but as our true spiritual nature.

We are a unique expression of Love. Love doesn't move through us. We are Love Loving Itself.

Light doesn't pass through us. We are Light.

We are the Abundance of God in action. We are the presence of Kindness.

Looking in any mirror is a good thing. Stand in front of the profile, the mirror, the belief system, and be grateful for the information.

But also be grateful that you are more than what can ever be seen with the human senses, or reflected in a human mirror of any kind.

Never born and never dying; we are rewriting the story we live in and what appears as life in matter.

As we do this, it becomes more and more apparent that there are not two universes, material and spiritual. Just one. Spiritual. We are not material. We are Spiritual.

We use human tools to discover this. Reflections of all kinds—mirrors, profiles, books, people, nature—reflect both our beliefs and Truth.

And as we learn this, we can celebrate what we know about ourselves and be grateful for the chance to play this earth game, because not playing will not make it go away.

Seeing through it is the answer.

All of this is why we are tracking what we say to ourselves about ourselves. Why we pay attention to our habits—moving them closer to spiritually healthy habits.

We pay attention to what we accept about what others say about us. Is it a clue, or a mistaken perception?

And in the end, here's where we are going. We are letting go of everything that describes us humanly, even the good stuff.

As we do this, we must be patient with ourselves, kind to ourselves, and enjoy the process. As they say in yoga classes, "Don't wish for this moment to be over." Be present. Receive the gift that the moment is offering.

In big R Reality, we have never left what we have called heaven. All we are doing now is letting go of what's hiding our present perfection from us, which is only a mistaken perception.

In the meantime, let's follow the wisdom of the Arab saying attributed to Mohammad, "Trust in Allah (God, the Divine, the Essence, Love), but tie up your camel."

Before we head into choosing your Right Identity statement, let's do more with the tool of Face and Replace, and then we'll check in with Sally.

FACE AND REPLACE: QUALITY WORD LISTS

We've been noticing how we identify ourselves and how others see us. Now, it's time to claim our true Spiritual identity.

Everyone has one, so don't try sneaking out of this.

Each of us is a unique expression of the Divine. Each of us has gifts that are the essence of our being. They are not something we have to earn. They are like the fragrance of a flower, the slow, steady rhythm of a turtle, the sweet song of the robin. They are part of us.

All of nature naturally expresses its gifts. Except for humans. Crazy, right? Instead, we deny what comes naturally to us, suppress it, run from it, or misuse it.

This book isn't about why we do that. I'm not sure it matters. What matters is that we notice it and shift it.

This book is about a practice that will dissolve that habit, belief, perception, and let our unique spiritual blessings shine forth.

Our next tool for doing this is something I call Quality Word lists. The concept is simple. Replace negative beliefs and thoughts about ourselves with positive qualities.

Remember, what we perceive to be reality magnifies, so why not?

However, we aren't making these up or wishing for them. We are noticing what's already present. They are already our gifts, our essence, but we've been denying or ignoring them.

What if a beautiful red rose started acting and thinking like a human and believed that it was ugly, dull, useless, and prickly? We could easily see that it is mistaken. Its essence is beauty, the color red, and sweet fragrance.

We are the same. Our qualities are baked into who we are. We only have to stop acting and thinking like a human. Yes, I laughed here. You can, too, if you want too. But we can do it! And we will.

To help us along, we'll use the Quality Word list tool as part of our Face and Replace process.

There are two kinds of quality lists that we could make, the qualities of how something looks and the qualities of feelings.

In this Right Thinking practice, we will focus on feeling qualities.

These qualities will help us bring our state of mind perception into harmony with our point of view.

Each quality is one word that contains the essence of what we mean.

If it takes a sentence to describe it, keep feeling it, and pare it down to one word. No one but us needs to understand what we mean by that quality.

It's a feeling, and trying to explain it brings it back into the human element which is extremely limited.

The question to answer is: *If I were the identity that I am claiming, how would I feel?*

If you haven't done this before, this may take some time to sink in. Allow yourself to feel how wonderful that would be.

We'll be making a second list, too.

We will make a Quality Word list that directly replaces the negative things we have heard about ourselves with a positive quality.

Let's see what Sally does with this perception shifting tool.

Sally's Identity Story

This week Sally felt a little better, although saying she was already healthy still felt like a lie most of the time. Especially if she looked in the mirror or got upset with herself for only being able to walk around the block a few times.

But it was beginning to make sense to Sally that it was what she had been saying to herself, or others said about her, or the worldview, that had kept her in the habit of not doing healthy things for herself.

The I Choose tool for Facing and Replacing helped her see those habits as thoughts first and then choosing different ones seemed too easy to do to make a difference. But it seemed to work.

So Sally decided to make her choices more specific. She did an I Choose list that began with *I Choose to walk every day.*

She couldn't believe how many things she had unconsciously put in the way of doing what she wanted to do. Things from not having the right shoes, not having enough time, to what would people think.

It was a long list, but Sally kept consciously choosing. She chose to have the right shoes, to have enough time, and to have people support her choices.

Doing nothing other than Consciously Choosing, she started walking and loving it. Mostly.

But sometimes she wondered what good it would do. However, once she recognized that it was also a habit of thinking, she went right back to the Right Thinking steps and Consciously Choosing.

Sally found that when she said to herself that since God was Health Itself, and she was a reflection and expression of God, it meant that she was already healthy and that kept her in the right frame of mind to keep going.

As Sally got ready to claim her Right Identity, she realized she had already been doing that by saying she was God's reflection and expression.

That's when Sally realized that every step of Right Thinking was embedded within each other.

That doing these simple exercises would change her health seemed impossible to her, but Sally was determined to do it. She had started this process, and she would finish it.

She was ready to use the second Face and

Replace tool, Quality Word lists, so she started with a list about how she would feel if she were healthy.

One thing she knew was if she felt healthy, she would feel free. So she wrote that word down on her list. It was a beginning, and strangely, she felt freer just by starting her Quality Word list.

And that feeling started bringing up more feelings, and as she distilled those feelings into qualities, Sally felt as if this practice might actually work.

Sally also started her second list that would replace the opposite of what she had noticed about what she said and thought about herself.

This list was easier for Sally. To replace loser, she wrote "winner." To replace the negative idea of being too picky she wrote "precise."

Sally enjoyed making these lists and decided it was the same as designing a room. Take out the old furniture and bring in the new.

Here's what Sally wrote down to continue her practice.

Overall Right Intent: *Get my health back.*
Right Intent: *To feel better.*
Right Premise: *I am already healthy and I feel great.*
Right Identity: *I am the expression of health.*

Change It

To answer the question, can I change my Right Thinking choices?

The quick answer is yes, of course.

Even though this is called Right Thinking, there is no right or wrong way to do it. I call this a thoughtful system, not a Right System, or the only way to do it system.

I expect us to keep thinking, wondering, and asking questions.

Think of this book as a path with signs that help you get where you are going.

However, once you know the territory and the habit of listening to the still small voice kicks in, you might find yourself mixing up the order, or using just one of the steps, or changing the words in each step every time.

I often find myself starting with one Intent or Premise or Identity and then changing them every time I repeat them.

Let that happen. Follow your internal guidance.

As long as we begin from our highest understanding of the Divine at each step, it is still Right Thinking.

I rarely keep the same wording twice. But that's because I have practiced walking myself through all the steps so many times it has become second nature.

Once you get the hang of this system and hear those Angel Ideas, change as needed.

When you feel grounded in the Principles of this practice, get out on that dance floor and dance!

However, taking one focus all the way through can be very powerful, and that's what we are doing here.

That said, let's review how your practice went this week.

Practical Identity:

It's time to claim your true spiritual nature. Intent, then Premise, and now Identity.

And yes, we keep writing them out. Writing things down over and over again helps override the programming that says otherwise.

Step Three: Right Identity

My overall intent for reading this book:

My Right Intent:

My Right Premise:

My Right Identity:

- Continue noticing how you are self identifying, and how others see you.

- Keep your I Choose sheets going for anything that you are working on.

- Start your Quality Word list to replace the negative things you hear about yourself.

- Start a Quality Word list about how you would feel if what you chose as your Right Identity were true.

- Choose at least one way that you will calm your thinking, quiet your mind and bring it into harmony with your intent. Do a meditation. Walk by yourself. Sit in nature. Listen to bird songs. Breathe.

Identity Review

Before we head into the next week's Right Thinking step, take a moment and review what happened in the past week.

As always, don't skip this step. Remember, it's what we don't notice that drives our life without our consciously choosing it.

Reviewing the week helps ground the work into something tangible, and although our intents are not measurable, progress is. Even if the progress doesn't feel good, note that, too. Everything is relevant for shifting our perceptions.

Things I noticed:

Ways I am stuck:

Things that have changed:

CHAPTER NINE: RESISTANCE

A sinner is not reformed merely by assuring him that he cannot be a sinner because there is no sin. To put down the claim of sin, you must detect it, remove the mask, point out the illusion, and thus get the victory over sin and so prove its unreality. —Mary Baker Eddy

We all know about resistance. Usually, we think of it as that quality that keeps us from doing something. We talk about resistance as a negative and work on overcoming it.

But what about good resistance? Yes, resistance has a positive side.

We resist the urge to put our hand on a hot stove, or run in front of a car, or say hurtful things on purpose. These are examples of good resistance.

So obviously, there are two ways to look at resistance—two kinds of resistance—the kind we say no to and the kind we say yes to.

We say no to the resistance that stops us from doing what we love to do, or want to do, or must do.

That is the kind of resistance that we want to overcome.

But here's the thing.

It's still a form of good resistance because our unconscious mind thinks it's working on our behalf. And it will continue to do so until we change what we believe to be true about ourselves and others.

We can't blame resistance for doing what we have asked it to do. Instead, we have to change ourselves so that resistance supports our genuine desires rather than thwarting them.

Intent, Premise, and Identity put us on the path to accomplishing that shift. By Consciously Choosing these first three steps, we gain insights into what we believe and accept as accurate about ourselves, others, and the world.

These first three steps in Right Thinking help us break habits that hold us back or keep us in stasis and the status quo.

Without changing our belief systems and habits, resistance works on our behalf to keep us stuck because it thinks that's what we want.

Therefore, it's obvious what we have to do. Shift our beliefs and habits to ones that work in our favor.

To make this kind of shift takes practice.

We practice setting spiritually healthy habits.

We practice overcoming paradigms, biases, and prejudices that hold us back or take us in a direction that is not safe, healthy, or happiness producing.

What we want to notice at all times is what we're resisting and why.

Are we resisting the call to move us into a clearer understanding of our true spiritual nature?

Let's say no to that resistance.

And we use yes resistance or Right Resistance to do so.

We are saying yes to learning how to resist what we need to resist. Not passively. But with conviction—the stomping our foot kind of resistance.

We use Right Resistance to not give into unhealthy temptations.

Yes, it's tempting to give in to temptations. It takes Right Resistance to say no to them, to call temptation a liar. That is the kind of resistance that we want.

We say yes to resisting lies, and liars, and doing harmful things to ourselves and others.

In the Say Yes class that I teach, we have discovered that saying no needs to happen more often than saying yes.

We can't say yes to what we want unless we make room for it.

That means we have to take the time to discover what is most important to us and say no to anything tempting us away from it.

In this book, that's what we did first; we set our Right Intent.

In doing so, we actively and consciously chose what is important to us—from how we make our beds to how we want to make our "mark" in the world.

Then we chose what Right Premise and Right Identity we need to stand in to make room for it to happen.

It is a practice of adjusting and refining our state of mind and point of view.

In this book, we are taking the time to look at ourselves to see what is coloring our perception. What paradigm, what belief systems are driving our lives without our being aware of them?

We are breaking the habit of staying in false, or no longer useful, perceptions about ourselves (which always overflows to others).

We are facing and replacing them with an improved version. This is Right Resistance.

And as our understanding grows, we continue to repeat this process over and over again. We replace what isn't true with quality words that are the essence of ourselves as expressions and reflections of the Divine.

We face and replace anything that claims evil has more power than Good. We face and replace the belief that we are anything less than the perfect representation of that Good.

Right Thinking is a skill that must be practiced and used every day and in every moment. Because as long as we exist in what we believe to be a human form, we must practice.

Spirituality is not magic.

We can't sprinkle fairy dust and have it change everything. However, we can imagine that fairy dust is God's essence, and that will shift our perception. So do it, but do it consciously, holding to a correct Intent, Premise, and Identity as you do so.

We have to practice resisting the temptations that are always around us. To do so, we can use the mirrors we have set up. They can alert us to what the temptations might be for us. They give us clues about the language that the liar speaks that will appeal to our human self.

That way, when we encounter these temptations, we will recognize them as temptations trying to pull us away from our True Identity.

Christ Jesus was tempted three times. He was tempted to put himself in danger so that God's angels would save him. He was tempted to declare himself King, in other words, claim human power. And he was tempted to worship false gods, to put his faith in what he knew was not true.

He used Right Resistance to say no. He claimed his True Intent, Premise, and Identity, showing us that we can do the same thing.

Yes, this is yes resistance in action. Right Resistance is when we say, "I resist what is not true."

And once we claim our Right Intent, Premise, and Identity, this gets much easier.

We are looking at error not to focus on it and have a conversation with it, but to replace it with what is True.

The kind of resistance that looks like war or fighting will never work in the long run because it is not replacing the error with Truth.

Our form of resistance is to remove the mask of all lies, beliefs, perceptions, temptations, and then throw the water of Truth, the light of the Divine on them, and let anything unlike Good dissolve away into nothingness.

Go forth, put on the armor of Truth, and resist temptation by shifting the story about yourself and the world to one that is only about the power of Good.

Whose Voice

Since for Right Resistance to work, we need to recognize which voice is telling us the truth, let's look at the ways we can tell them apart.

Temptation that takes us away from our true nature always—not sometimes—always disguises itself as a voice we will trust.

Its favorite disguise is to "speak" to us in the same way we talk and think. It has to choose this method, because the only substance it has is our belief in it.

Which means even the most aware person can sometimes be confused or fooled.

However, once we know it's not God's voice speaking, we can stop listening, stop being curious, stop obeying. It will be easy when we claim for ourselves that all that really exists is Love.

To make the recognition easier, here are eleven ways to tell which voice is speaking.

There is the Angel voice reminding you of your true spiritual nature, let's call that voice God, or the Devil voice wanting to stop you from knowing big T Truth.

- 1. It's not God when you say or think: "This is the way I am."

God has placed no limits on who we are and what we do.

God does not know us as human creations that fit within categories.

It is our human sense of ourselves that states we can only be one way and not the other.

When the voice says, "You are too shy to do that," or "You are good at that but not this," or "You are too young, too old, a mother, a father, a woman, a man, a sister, a brother" or any other description that is limiting it is not God's voice.

We are all the full and unlimited expression of the Infinite One called God. Limitation is not God speaking.

It is God when you hear, "You are free from that limitation."

- 2. It's not God when it is based on conditional, biased Love.

God does not judge.

It is our human sense of God that has made God into a parody of our humanness. We have made a god in our likeness.

But like the sun which shines on all equally, God, as Infinite Love, loves equally. We do not have to meet any material conditions to be loved.

When we act out from a human understanding of God, we may find ourselves judging, wishing or wanting, feeling hate, sorrow or revenge. However, conditions and judgment are not God.

It is God when you hear, "Only Love and Love only."

•3. It's not God when you hear, "why bother, nothing I do makes a difference."

You have a unique talent that must be expressed.

Feelings that no one will notice or appreciate it, or that the world can do without it, are a blatant lie.

God is all there is to Life. We are all necessary for the fullness of God to be expressed.

Since it would be impossible for God to not be expressing Itself, in Truth we, too, are always expressing our unique talent.

Once you stop listening to the "Devil" the world will unfold new and wonderful ways for you to be noticed and make a difference. Do them; you are the only one who can!

It is God when you hear, "Live your gift."

•4. It's not God when you are hoping for a material outcome.

Since God is eternal unlimited Spirit, what does It know of matter or our material needs? Nothing!

Using God to improve our lives is a sham. We are only fooling ourselves and keeping our true supply and wealth from appearing.

Understanding God as All immediately reveals what was hidden in plain sight. What is revealed is all that we need and more than we imagine.

It is God when you hear, "I already provided what you need, just notice."

•5. It's not God when you are intent on improving the situation your way.

Human ego is not God.

If you think about it, nothing ever turns out as you planned. In fact, when letting go and letting God, it turned out better than you could have ever thought.

Demanding the outcome you want is not of God.

The human sense of existence will never produce an answer that blesses all, as it always comes from ego and duality. Infinite Mind is constantly unfolding blessings beyond our comprehension because it is One.

It is God when you hear, "Surrender to being loved and cared for now."

•6. It's not God when it requires any form of deceit or manipulation.

In our belief of being human, it's hard to imagine that things can't happen without our intervention.

We forget that nobody is really human, and that everybody is as much an expression of God as we are, and just as capable of being guided and directed by that awareness.

Trying to make it work is not God.

It is God when you hear, "Trust in Love."

•7. It's not God when it claims that one person, sex, or race is better than another.

Claiming a sense of worthiness based on a privileged position through circumstances has nothing to do with God.

Within Love's eyes, there are no categories to place anyone at a different level.

Sometimes it is our sense of personal human unworthiness that makes us claim that we are better than others.

Sometimes this claim is subtle, as in "I am glad I don't look that old" and sometimes it is horribly abusive, as in any kind of war.

In no case is it God. God knows no classes, states, or categories.

It is God when you hear, "All that exists expresses who I AM."

•8. It's not God when it berates, undermines, depresses, or abuses anyone—including you.

The commandment, "Thou shall not kill," is not just referring to the human body, but also to the spirit.

For example, when someone says, "You can't do anything right, or you are not worth it, or you belong to me, or I can do that much better than you," they are killing the Spirit.

And that is not God speaking.

God as perfect Love expands and unfolds the Spirit. Imagine what it would feel like to be perfectly loved. Obviously there is no room at all for anything hateful in Love.

It is God when you hear, "I AM Love Loving Itself."

•9. It's not God when you feel pushed or threatened.

If we agree with the worldview that there is not enough time, money, patience, love or any other suggestion of lack, then feeling pushed or threatened might feel normal.

However, God is Infinite All. This means there is no possibility of any kind of lack. God need not push or threaten, instead It guides by existing only as Love.

It is God when you hear, "Peace be still."

•10. It's not God when it makes you feel apathetic or indifferent.

Sometimes we think it would be better if we "left well enough alone."

And yet some of the greatest evils of the human world have been caused by our indifference or looking the other way, or saying "I don't care, or what difference would that make?"

One of the "Devil's" greatest tools is our apathy to its claims.

You acting as the expression of Love will leave no room for apathy or indifference.

It is God when you hear, "Be active in Love."

- 11. It's not God if you are thinking, "what about me?"
-

****

This doesn't mean that we are not to be wise about what we need to do to take care of ourselves. It doesn't mean that we should give away all our light, leaving none for ourselves.

What it means is to not let our ego and self-centered needs guide what we say, think or do.

There is no need to make the statement "what about me" when our intention is to live completely in each moment in the awareness of God.

That awareness brings all that we need. Me is not God. There is only I AM.

It is God when you hear, "Serve others in My name."

If we pay attention, we'll realize that there really is no "you" that is thinking.

It is either God or the belief of the Devil. We are either expressing God or we are allowing ourselves to be the tool of the Devil.

All it takes is the willingness to shift our perception to big R Reality, and the discipline to not focus on magnifying the outward material circumstances.

The time that it takes for what appears to be a change to occur may seem to vary. Remember, no matter what your sense perception tries to tell you, no matter what prison it attempts to send you to, it is always a lie about who you are and what is happening, when it does not reflect and express Infinite Good, Love.

Let's see how Sally is doing with Right Resistance.

Sally's Right Resistance

Sally's growing awareness that all the Right Thinking steps are embedded within each other prepared her for this next step, Right Resistance.

After reading about Right Resistance, Sally realized that the I Choose sheets and Quality Word lists were already helping her with Right Resistance. She was overcoming the resistance that kept her from being who she wanted to be.

However, one day nothing went right. She spilled soup all over the floor. Forgot to go to an appointment and realized she hadn't gone for a walk in the last three days.

That's when she noticed that the voice in her head that told her what a loser she had always been and always would be might not be telling her the truth.

Sally had always accepted that the voice in her head was herself talking to herself, which meant, of course, she listened. How could she not? It was loud. It spoke like her. And it told her things she had always believed.

Learning that it wasn't her voice, or God's voice, was a game-changer. Sally felt that it would be possible to heal all the situations and problems in her life.

A new hope arose in Sally. Perhaps, it really was possible to change the story of her life.

Sally got serious about collecting quality words about herself. When she heard a negative version, she reversed it, found a quality word for it, and added it to her list.

She imagined herself as healthy and then asked herself how she would feel if she were healthy. After some practice and deep listening, she got the hang of narrowing all of her feelings down to one word. It was like packing a hundred feelings into a word.

Sally had two lists going.

One list was for reversing all the negative things she said or thought about herself. This list had words like diligent, to counter the belief she was lazy, and the word compassionate to dispute the judgment of herself and others that she often felt.

The second list was how she would feel if she were perfectly healthy. That list included quality words like relieved and joyous.

Sally figured she would keep the two lists going, not worrying about how long they were.

She had been listening and believing the negative for so long she knew it would take time to unravel. Besides, Sally wanted to get better at discovering, accepting, and living as her true Spiritual nature.

Here's what Sally wrote to continue her practice.

Overall Right Intent: *Get my health back.*
Right Intent: *To feel better.*
Right Premise: *I am already healthy and I feel great.*
Right Identity: *I am the expression of health.*
Right Resistance: *I resist ungodly temptations.*

PRACTICAL RESISTANCE:

This only takes a minute or two to fill out. But writing it out, repeatedly, helps to rewrite the story more effectively. Resist the urge to not do the assignments anymore.

Human personality, ego, worldview, does not want to go away. It will find many ways to stop you from cleaning up your old and limiting perceptions.

Don't fall for its tricks. Remember, anything that doesn't move you toward your true Spiritual nature is not your friend. Keep going!

This is our foundation. The next two steps Practice and Action will keep our house sturdy and safe.

STEP FOUR: RIGHT RESISTANCE

My overall intent for reading this book:

My Right Intent:

My Right Premise:

My Right Identity:

My Right Resistance

- Continue noticing how you are self identifying, and how others see you.

- Keep your I Choose sheets going for anything that you are working on.

- Do your Quality Word list to replace the negative things you hear about yourself.

- Do a Quality Word list about how you would feel if what you chose as your Right Resistance were true.

- Choose at least one way that you will calm your thinking, quiet your mind and bring it into harmony with your intent. Do a meditation. Walk by yourself. Sit in nature. Listen to bird songs. Breathe.

Resistance Review

Before we head into the next week's Right Thinking step, take a moment and review what happened in the past week.

As always, don't skip this step. Remember, it's what we don't notice that drives our life without our consciously choosing it.

Reviewing the week helps ground the work into something tangible, and although our intents are not measurable, progress is. Even if the progress doesn't feel good, note that too. Everything is relevant for shifting our perceptions.

Things I noticed:

Ways I am stuck:

Things that have changed:

Chapter Ten: Reasoning

It is a capital mistake to theorize before one has data. Insensibly one begins to twist facts to suit theories, instead of theories to suit facts. —Arthur Conan Doyle

I bet you saw this chapter's heading "Right Reasoning" and realized that we have been doing this all along. And yes, you are right! We have been reasoning following a logical train of thought.

If this is that, then that is this, and then this is the outcome. Right? Yes, that sounds a bit confusing, so let's walk through what we have been doing and see if it makes more sense.

We started with the theory that what we perceive to be reality magnifies.

I call it a theory, but since no one has proved that it's not true, and we have many proofs it is, we choose that point of view as our beginning. Everything else flows from that point of view.

(If you want more on why I believe the theory is true, I write it out in detail in my book *Living In Grace: The Shift To Spiritual Perception.* Or read the first chapter of *Genesis.*)

Since it's true, it makes perfect sense to choose our point of view based on what we want to magnify, see, and experience in our lives. We are always choosing the best point of view that we can, because—well, why not?

We get what we believe and we see what we believe. Therefore, it's a wise idea to believe the best scenario possible. I am sure you agree.

Then we explored the idea that emotions and feelings drive our perception and therefore, what we experience, so we added ways to get our state of mind in harmony with our point of view.

To review, here's an example of what this looks like:

We chose a perception that there is one divine Intelligence ruling all creation.

We know that there can only be one Creator, and we know that this Intelligence has to be all good or all bad, so we chose good because we realize that all bad would have long ago destroyed itself.

Next, we accepted that we are the expression, children, reflection of God, or Good, so our identity and experience can only comprise good.

We put this in terms that our human self can use practically. We set an Intent.

I didn't have to tell you to make it one that reflected all Good. You did that automatically. I knew you would. I'm not a mind reader, but I know that you wouldn't be reading this book if you didn't already want to express only good in your own way in the world.

After setting your Right Intent, you accepted that the intent is supported and guided by Divine Intelligence. That's your premise.

It's the same as saying, "I can do this because God is the only power, and that power is Love."

The next part is straightforward to reason out. Since there is only one God, one creator, one power, and you and I are the unique expression, reflection, action of that One power, we can state our Right Identity in those terms as a fact, as in "I am the expression, presence, of Love."

Next, we looked at what tries to tell us that none of this is true, and we resisted what it said. We called it a liar.

Interestingly, what comes up for most of us is that even though we have said that we are all the expression of the Divine, we think it might be true for every other person in the entire world, but not for us.

That is the human ego, personality, talking. You know what it's claiming, right? That we are God or gods. Wow. I know for sure that's not true. The world is most definitely not held in the palm of my hand. Or yours.

That is the best news ever. We are not God or gods. We are the action of One God. Or, as Mary Baker Eddy says, we are the compound idea of God.

If, and when, we allow ourselves to accept that somehow we escaped God's ever-expanding intelligent and all-encompassing Love and created ourselves and our lives outside of it; we are accepting a lie.

But it's tempting to believe it because that sure makes us unique, doesn't it?

However, if you figure out how that makes sense—how we can be outside of the One creation, let me know.

Otherwise, instead of agreeing with that lie about our identity, we don't agree. We use Right Resistance. We throw the lie out the door of our thinking.

I know, like a stalker, it comes back. Sometimes it pounds on the door or slips in a crack. It loves to remind us of all our mistakes—the stupid things we have said and done. As humans, we do all that, it's true.

As expressions of the Divine, we have done none of it, and that is the point of view and state of mind that we want to magnify.

And this is when Right Reasoning kicks in and we remember that anything that claims a power other than God is a lie.

There is only one liar, and it tells one lie, that there is a creator and power other than the one God, Good.

Accepting as a fact that we have power, that we created a situation, that we are bad, is agreeing with the liar. Let's not do that!

However, we have to let go of our human ego-self because the human ego is an idiot. I call myself an idiot at least once a day. I get upset over not being perfect or making mistakes.

But that doesn't mean that I can't face and replace that with the reminder that I, like you, am already the perfect expression of the Divine. I am not the human self or my personality.

Right Reasoning carries us away from the turmoil of humanness. It shelters us, takes us higher, brings us into the realm where we can see the light of Truth.

It is only the human ego that claims we are separate, that we are alone. The human ego that thinks people have to go through us to hear God's word. Not true. Everyone is a direct expression of God. We are equal and together as unique expressions of the Divine.

Yes, all of this takes practice, and yes, that's our next step. For now, just listen. Truth is always speaking directly to you.

What voice are you listening to?

Reason it out. Which one lifts you into the state of mind of heaven, and which one talks to the human personality?

That is Right Reasoning.

We all know this prayer. It's a perfect example of reasoning it out, especially when combined with Mary Baker Eddy's added definition.

Our Father which art in heaven,
    Our Father-Mother God, all-harmonious,

Hallowed be Thy name.
    Adorable One.

Thy kingdom come.
    Thy kingdom is come; Thou art ever-present.

Thy will be done in earth, as it is in heaven.
    Enable us to know,—as in heaven, so on earth,—God is omnipotent, supreme.

Give us this day our daily bread;
    Give us grace for to-day; feed the famished affections;

And forgive us our debts, as we forgive our debtors.

And Love is reflected in Love;

And lead us not into temptation, but deliver us from evil;

And God leadeth us not into temptation, but delivereth us from sin, disease, and death.

For Thine is the kingdom, and the power, and the glory, forever.

For God is infinite, all-power, all Life, Truth, Love, over all, and All.

Let's see how Sally does with this idea of Right Reasoning.

Sally's Right Reasoning

When Sally read about Right Reasoning, she laughed. Wasn't this what she had been doing all along? *This Right Thinking was getting easier,* she thought. All she had to do was focus on how she reasoned for the next week and see how she could improve.

She liked the idea of "arguing" for the Right side of things. Sally decided to pretend that she was a defense attorney.

She would spend the week defending herself with logical reasoning, against anything that tried to tell her she was a loser.

Halfway through the first day, Sally realized that she was going to be a very busy attorney. That voice in her head never stopped with the blaming.

It told her she was a loser in almost every way imaginable, to how she cleaned her house and how she ate. And it always had proof.

After all, all she had to do was look in the mirror, home, or relationships. *Who did that to themselves and their life*, that voice asked. *It was you*, it said, and Sally knew that was true.

The prosecuting attorney's claims of how she was guilty of being a loser was prolific. It claimed that everything wrong in her life was her fault, from the cold she caught last month to her cluttered home and neglected friends and family.

Because there was an element of truth in what the voice said, it was tempting for Sally to agree that she was a loser.

But she was unwilling to continue to live her life this way, so she claimed her innocence. She was not guilty.

But how could she be not guilty? What the voice claimed she had and had not done was correct.

That's when Sally realized that Right Reasoning couldn't start with the outcome of a problem, or even with the problem, because if she did, she would be stopped in her tracks. All around her was the evidence of her guilt.

Sally started to understand why it is necessary to begin with a point of view that negates all of the human picture.

She couldn't fix everything by staying in the human version of the problem. She had to step outside of it, rise above it, and begin with the point of view that she was the perfect expression of Infinite Mind.

Just because the human picture had become muddled and messed up didn't change the Truth, Sally reasoned. *If she started with Truth, the human situation would improve.*

Sally understood that this was the only permanent way out of the mess, so she decided to choose the Truth about her true Spiritual nature as her point of view.

She was determined to stand in that Truth to defend herself. She would not resort to arguing about the human problem.

Part of Sally didn't believe this would work. But since she had been trying all her life to become a better human, and not doing a great job of it, she asked herself, why not try it?

So she stood her ground against the prosecutor's claims. She claimed her innocence. She claimed her true spiritual nature. She told the prosecutor that the human story and the human picture wasn't the one that was true about her. She would not accept it.

Sally used the I Choose and Quality Words tools to Face and Replace everything. At first, it felt as if nothing changed, except she felt better about herself.

But as the week went on, Sally could see how she was gaining ground over the voice. There were even moments when she didn't hear it anymore, or it was so quiet she could ignore it.

Yes, Sally decided. *This might actually work.*

Here is Sally's blueprint for Right Thinking:

Overall Right Intent: *Get my health back.*
Right Intent: *To feel better.*
Right Premise: *I am already healthy and I feel great.*
Right Identity: *I am the expression of health.*
Right Resistance: *I resist ungodly temptations.*
Right Reasoning: *I am not the human picture.*

Practical Reasoning

Here's this week's assignments. All for you. Keep that in mind, just in case you feel like skipping this part.

This only takes a minute or two to fill out. But writing it out, repeatedly, helps to rewrite the story more effectively.

Step Five: Right Reasoning

My overall intent for reading this book:

My Right Intent:

My Right Premise:

My Right Identity:

My Right Resistance:

My Right Reasoning:

- Continue noticing how you are self identifying, and how others see you.

- Keep your I Choose sheets going for anything that you are working on.

- Continue your Quality Word list to replace the negative things you hear about yourself.

- Continue a Quality Word list about how you would feel if what you chose as your Right Reasoning were true.

- Choose at least one way that you will calm your thinking, quiet your mind and bring it into harmony with your intent. Do a meditation. Walk by yourself. Sit in nature. Listen to bird songs. Breathe.

REASONING REVIEW

Before we head into the next week's Right Thinking step, take a moment and review what happened in the past week.

Don't skip this step. Remember, it's what we don't notice that drives our life without our consciously choosing it.

Reviewing the week helps ground the work into something tangible, and although our intents are not measurable, progress is.

Even if the progress doesn't feel good, note that too. Everything is relevant for shifting our perceptions.

Things I noticed:

Ways I am stuck:

Things that have changed:

Chapter Eleven: Practice

I am the tool with which God works. My virtue is to participate in this work, and I can do so if I keep the instrument which is given to me, namely my soul, in immaculate condition. —Leo Tolstoy

This step is an easy one. We've been talking about it all along. There is nothing new to do.

All we have to do is practice what we have already learned. And then practice some more. And enjoy the practice, because everything we love to do takes practice.

No one woke up one day, threw the perfect pot, danced like Baryshnikov, sang like Pavarotti, or knew things like Richard Feynman. No one. Not even them.

What does everyone have in common? Practice.

We are practicing to be life artists. As Henry David Thoreau said, *To affect the quality of the day, that is the highest of arts.*

We are practicing to overcome the belief that we are humans tied to material beliefs and conditions.

We are practicing to understand our true spiritual nature and live it to the best of our ability. We practice learning how to enjoy it and share it.

Whenever I think of practice, I think about the practice of ballet. Ballet is a practice that has been around for hundreds of years. Every day, ballet practitioners do a daily ballet class.

Every class begins with a barre routine that every ballet teacher follows. That means we could take ballet in Pennsylvania, and then in California or Paris, and do the same barre.

All over the world, the same set of steps in the same order. The only difference might be in the style or the twist the teacher adds to the practice.

Every discipline has this kind of practice.

What makes our daily practice different is that we get to set that routine for ourselves. So, what does your daily practice look like for you?

To design your own best practice, you need to know yourself and what you desire, and that's what we have been doing all along, isn't it?

To be life artists, we can't escape the need for practice to achieve awareness and wisdom. This practice is flexible, as it should be because this practice is knowing and understanding the Divine, which is the epitome of infinite ways to do something.

Of course, we intend to practice this in every moment, but we need to set times and studies and lessons to shift our point of view and state of mind until we live in it at all times.

We have to be willing to let go of what we have outgrown and no longer need. Whether represented by things or thoughts or habits, if it doesn't fit what we have become, let it go.

We don't keep the clothes we wore when we were ten, thinking we might wear them again someday.

Similarly, we need not keep outgrown ideas around thinking we might want to be that person again someday. Let them go.

Another type of practice is being good at what we want to do in our life.

If we desire to be a writer, we have to study writing, practice writing, practice reading, and practice listening to teachers about the art of writing. Practice expressing ourselves.

This is true, no matter what we desire to do with our days. Practice getting better at it. Do it your way, but practice.

Sometimes the practice may be sitting quietly every day in meditation. Or practice learning new technology.

Practice not agreeing with limitations imposed upon us through world, family, and friend's beliefs.

Even when these beliefs are meant well, and they often are, we still get to choose. Does it fit where we want to go and who we want to be?

Then we can practice being kind in our refusal to agree. We can do what needs to be done, but without spreading anger and grief.

When we study nature, we see how each element of nature is unique and yet fits together. Nature is diverse. Each bug, bird, animal, plant is living a life that serves a purpose and connects with every other living thing on our planet.

How many people live on earth? Each one of us is different, and yet we are the same. Even if you and I are doing the same job, we will bring our strengths and style to it.

Back to the ballet barre. Same barre. Everyone does it, intending to make every movement perfect. At the barre, everyone looks the same. The intent is to get to do the movements as correctly as possible. Each practice step is designed to strengthen muscles and make them flexible at the same time.

After the barre, it's time for action. The last half of the class is spent moving across the floor, putting into practice the barre's skills. Of course, each step in the second half of the class is also the same everywhere.

After that, a dancer gets to practice a choreographed dance. Why? To perform it. To share.

And then, each person takes the practice and expresses it in their unique way. The more they have practiced, the more they have eliminated what isn't needed, the more willing they are to be present, the more their unique self shines through.

I have used ballet as an example. Not only because I know it, but because it is one of the most rigid practices that I have ever taken part in.

You'd think that only rigidity would come out of that. And yet, that's not what happens. Individuality does. Even non-ballet dancers (like me) take that same ballet barre. Why? Because of the structure of the practice.

The point of all this is to give you an example of why it is vital to design your practice structure. It may change in the seasons of your life. In fact, I am sure that it will.

But we always have that still small voice within to guide us. As we get more and more skilled at Right Thinking and quiet the loud monkey mind voice in our head, we will become more able to listen to the quiet voice. The voice that brings us Angel Ideas.

All six steps bring us to the next Right Thinking step—Right Action.

In the meantime, think about your practice. What does it look like for you?

Remember, we are not practicing to get better at old habits. We are making new ones. That's Right Practice.

Quality Word Practice

During the last few weeks, we have been using two tools to shift our thinking; I Choose sheets and Quality Word lists.

Once we finish an I Choose sheet, we are done—no need to look at it again. In fact, don't.

If you are still stuck, do another one. But looking through an old one is like picking up the garbage you just threw out and bringing it back into the house to study it.

Quality Words lists are a different story altogether. These we want to look at again. Quality words can act like our North star, keeping us focused on our true spiritual nature.

Quality words are taking things, turning them back into qualities of God—which they were in the first place. As a result, the original thing, situation, or idea will more accurately reflect its true spiritual nature too. Cool, right?

Look at your lists and see if you can narrow each list down to the top ten words. Now, here's what you do with them. If you have read my other books, you'll recognize this process, but it's always good to review it.

If this is new to you, you are in for a treat. After reviewing how to use your Quality Word list, we'll check in with Sally to see how she is doing.

How To Order Quality Word Lists

Using quality words, we will discover what we truly want. Often we'll find we already have it. We simply didn't recognize it because we were looking for the wrong thing.

All things are, in essence, composed of qualities.

When we translate things back into their qualities, a fantastic thing happens. We become conscious of what is already present for us. It may not look like we thought it would look like, but it will be what we wanted.

But first, we have to find out what our heart wants.

Quality Words will become a way of life once you experience the power of them. So, let's get started and make you an expert at using quality words to shift your life.

In this Right Thinking practice, you have made two lists.

- One list reversed the negative things you heard, or thought, about yourself. This list contains positive qualities. It is actually a list of what is true about your true spiritual nature.

- The second list is how you would feel if you were living your Right Thinking Intent.

Once you have both lists pared down to about ten Quality Words in each list, it's time to put them into order.

Yes, they are already in order. But they are in order based on how you thought about them. We need to put in them order based on how you feel about them.

Have you ever been at a place in your life where nothing happens towards what you want, no matter what you do? This is most likely because you have a quality or value block.

If we have two values that feel equal to us, our core-self will be confused about which one to provide.

Remember, our conversation about how state of mind overrides point of view? In the same way, what we feel overrides what we thought about as we made this list.

Yes, the heart rules the intellect—the feminine guides our masculine life.

This is not how it plays out most of the time in the worldview. We can see how well that works. It doesn't.

Doing this exercise will be a guide for your actions to follow your heart desires. It's one of the most powerful things we can do.

Remember, the order your lists end up in will not be the same order that your intellectual mind put them in while making them.

And you need someone to help you with this. You can't do it alone. But the person who helps you has to be in the same heart space that you are. If you can't find someone, let me know.

Once you find the person, both of you need to read the instructions listed below.

Once you understand the process, it becomes second nature, so take the time to let it sink in.

Quality Word lists not only work but are one of the most powerful and simple tools I know to shift lives.

Don't look at your list while your partner is working with you, as this will engage brain and logic. What you want to engage is your heart and inspiration.

Your partner will ask you the following question each time:

"Which is more important to you?" and will give you two words on the list to compare.

Your partner must not give you any other verbal or physical cues. Don't listen to anything except your inner voice. Respond with the answer it tells you. Don't argue with it.

If you cannot choose one as more important than the other, your partner should ask you, "Which one can you not live without?"

Notice that your mind tells you that if you choose one, you might not get the other. That fear comes from the point of view that there is never enough and that you don't deserve everything you want.

Since neither statement is true, notice these thoughts and move on. The truth is, once you are clear about what you desire to see, you will be able to see and receive all these qualities in a form appropriate for you.

Your partner must compare each word with every word until you have an ordered list. You will probably be surprised at the order if you have stayed with your heart and trusted your answers.

Here is how I do this.

(Don't worry, this is a step-by-step process. Easy. Don't let worry get in the way.)

Take a sheet of paper. Draw a line down the middle. Write your partner's original quality words on the left.

Put your finger on the first word on your partner's list. (This is so you don't lose your place.)

Ask the "which is more important" question by comparing the first word on the list to the second one. If they say the first word, move on to comparing the first word to the third word.

What if they say the second word is more important? Great. Cross it off and move it to the right side of the page.

Now compare the first word to the third word. If they say the first word is more important, move on.

What if they say the third word is more important than the first? Great. Cross it off.

But before you move it to the right side of the page, you have to find out if it is more important, or less important, than the word that is already over there.

So ask the "which is more important" question between those two words on the right.

Let's say the third word is more important than

the second, so write it above the second word.

Go back to the left side of the list. Your finger is still on that first word. Compare it to the fourth word, and so on down the list until you have done the entire left side of the list.

If you have found more words that are more important than the first one, they will go to the right side after you compare them to that list, from the bottom up.

For example, you have two words on the right. The third word is first, and then the second. Now you have a new word. Compare it to the second. If it is more important, compare it to the third. If it is more important, put it at the top. If it isn't, it goes in the middle.

(Here's where you realize you need lots of spaces between the words on the right because you never know where the list is going.)

After you have completed comparing the first word all the way down the list on the left, you will have some crossed-out words on the left because they are now on the right in their right order.

Cross out the first word and add it at the bottom of the list on the right.

Draw a line under that list. You are finished with those words.

Go to the list on the left. Put your finger on the first uncrossed out word. Compare it with the next uncrossed out word below it.

Do the same thing with the words that you did before.

When you are done doing that with the new words, put a line under the list and start again on the left.

Usually, this takes two or three passes. But keep going until all the words are crossed out on the left and in order on the right.

Now you can move on to how to use your list.

How To Use Your Quality Word List

Now that you have a quality word list, how do you use it? Of course, you could ignore it and hope things change. But now that you have put so much work into the list, why not make the most of it?

Here are the four simple ways to use your list. Use it and get ready to experience more than you might imagine.

•1. Use the qualities as a filter.

If something appears that you think might be what you are looking for and does not have at least the first four qualities—with the first one first and the rest following in order, it is not "it."

Think of the time you will save if you can eliminate quickly and easily what is not right for you.

For example, you discover that safety is first on your quality list for a means of transportation and the car you are looking at has a very low safety record, don't buy this car no matter how much you love it.

If you buy it, you will eventually be unhappy with it, and somehow you will unconsciously figure out how to get rid of it.

•2. See the qualities everywhere.

See the qualities in everything, not just in what you're seeking. Notice that they're always with you in many forms.

You have always had, and always will have, each quality on your list if you practice looking and expect to see it.

A quality does not have to belong to you. It can appear anywhere. All of what you see is your world. The goal is to notice that the quality you're looking for already exists everywhere, and since you can see it—it exists for you—now.

•3. Be grateful for each quality as you see it.

Be grateful for these qualities each time you see

them, no matter where they occur. If the person you dislike most has one of these qualities, be grateful that you have seen this quality in your life.

Know that if it is "out there" it was first "within here" and therefore always available, and always part of your life.

4. Be and live these qualities yourself.

I know that you are discovering that having the "thing" you wanted is no longer as important. You have found that it already exists as thoughts—qualities.

As we express gratitude for this, we have shifted our perception towards our Right Intent. The result?

Sometimes we realize we don't need the thing we were asking to see, or it turns up in another package, or it appears in a way more excellent than we could have dreamed.

Whichever way this happens, it will more closely match your Right Intent which cannot help but produce in your world whatever you need at the moment. You have always had it.

None of us have ever been abandoned, nor could we ever be. Looking for qualities opens our eyes to what has always been and always will be ours.

That changes everything.

A Note About Your Quality Words

Can you say, "I am" in front of each word on your what-is-true-about-me list?

If not, think about changing them to the form that allows you to do so. Otherwise, these words may describe what you do, and in Right Thinking, we are aiming for who you are—your essence.

These can be the same words, just a different form.

If you like the word in the form that it is, keep it that way. As always, this is your practice, and doing it how it works the best for you is the way to do it.

Sally's Right Practice

Five steps into Right Thinking, Sally realizes that she is not only feeling better about herself, she is feeling happier. So much so, she slacks off and forgets about the sixth step.

After all, things are better. Besides, it's hard to keep going, especially since she has been doing this all by herself.

A few days go by before Sally notices that the voice in her head is loud again. Even more so.

She hasn't looked at her quality words, and she hasn't defended herself. She has left her mental door open. At first, she feels guilty. Then she gets angry at herself.

That voice is right. She is a loser. Sally lets herself fall into that belief for a moment, but recognizes almost immediately that it's not a voice that wants to help her.

It wants to stop her from remembering and living her true spiritual identity.

She knows what to do. She quickly walks herself back through the steps. It's easy. She's been writing them down every week. She finds her latest list and repeats it to herself.

When she gets to the sixth step of Right Practice, she realizes why Right Thinking has to be an ongoing practice.

She can't let herself lapse back into old beliefs. Moving away from and staying out of them will take time and dedication.

At first, that idea is depressing. She would have to practice Right Thinking her whole life.

Didn't she get time off? Didn't everyone deserve a break?

When she heard the still small voice say, "But this is the break," something shifted in Sally's thinking, and she realized that staying in Right Thinking was a vacation from the human mess and drama that wanted to claim her days.

It was harder not to practice, than it was to practice.

With that awareness, Sally felt as if the weight of the world had fallen off her shoulders. In a very real sense, that was exactly what had happened.

Here is Sally's blueprint for Right Thinking:

Overall Right Intent: *Get my health back.*
Right Intent: *To feel better.*
Right Premise: *I am already healthy and I feel great.*
Right Identity: *I am the expression of health.*
Right Resistance: *I resist ungodly temptations.*
Right Reasoning: *I am not the human picture.*
Right Practice: *I practice with my quality words.*

Practical Practice

Here are this week's assignments. All for you. Keep that in mind, just in case you feel like skipping this part.

This only takes a minute or two to fill out. But writing it out, repeatedly, helps to rewrite the story more effectively.

Step Six: Right Practice

My overall intent for reading this book:

My Right Intent:

My Right Premise:

My Right Identity:

My Right Resistance:

My Right Reasoning:

My Right Practice:

- Continue noticing how you are self identifying, and how others see you.

- Keep your I Choose sheets going for anything that you are working on.

- Use your Quality Word lists to make decisions and shift perceptions.

- Choose at least one way that you will calm your thinking, quiet your mind and bring it into harmony with your intent. Do a meditation. Walk by yourself. Sit in nature. Listen to bird songs. Breathe.

Practice Review

Before we head into the next week's Right Thinking step, take a moment and review what happened in the past week.

It may seem like extra work, but it's not. Just keep the habit going, and you'll see how it all flows together.

Things I noticed:

Ways I am stuck:

Things that have changed:

Chapter Twelve: Action

I don't need time. What I need is a deadline.
—Duke Ellington

Action. I love this step. But it's so easy to skip. For so many reasons. Resistance, apathy, fear, confusion, status quo. But without action, all that we have done up to now is talk.

We all know people who talk about concepts and ideas but don't live them. We are not those people. We choose to walk our talk.

Yes, we have been doing Right Action all along, because as with all the steps, they go together.

Each step circles around each other. They switch places like the do-Si-do in a square dance. The steps aren't a straight line. They are a tapestry, a spiral, an evolving unfoldment.

That doesn't change the fact that it's easier to study something by laying it out and looking at it step by step, which is what we have done with these Seven Steps To Right Thinking.

I have Right Action last in line because to take Right Action we have had to put ourselves in the right state of mind and point of view.

Otherwise, we might not end up where we meant to go. Or we might take action we regret, only because we didn't pause first. We could drive down the wrong road, navigate the wrong river, take the wrong bus...well, you get the idea.

If we take the wrong road, float down the wrong river, or ride the wrong bus, we can get off at any time. We all make mistakes.

The only error worth worrying about is the one we are afraid to admit and correct. It would be like saying, "Oops, I missed my exit, so I'll keep driving down this road."

That's not what we do unless we want to go exploring. Instead, we get off, check where we meant to go, and head that way. So when we take action that doesn't turn out the way we intended, we can try something else until we end up where we meant to go.

Or more accurately, where our Right Intent, Premise, and Identity have designed us to go.

I think it's easier to deal with the step of action by breaking it down into little pieces. We know them as goals and to-dos.

For example, if we intend to communicate our message with clarity, then what is a goal? That would depend on each person's unique expression of the Divine.

My goal and your goal may be different, even if we have the same intent. And goals can change with the year, the day, the hour, the minute.

I know mine have. I have the same Right Intent for what I perceive as my Life Mission, but changing seasons of life result in in different goals and different to-dos.

For example, my goal at one point was to publish a new book every month. I know people that do that. I broke it down into to-do steps.

But I quickly discovered that goal didn't suit me. It didn't fit into a bigger context of other plans I had for fulfilling my intent.

Something had to change. So I changed my goal and the to-do steps. I didn't change my intent.

I am continually adjusting my goals to support my Right Intents and expand my perception and ability to experience joy.

Take one of your intents. Check and make sure it's not a goal.

Please go through the next steps to clarify what that intent is and have it based on your Truth. Then set a goal based on all that. Yes, there can be many goals based on your intent, but start with one. Then break it down into to-do steps.

And I do mean, break it down—tiny steps.

I use several tools to do this, slips of paper, teux deux, kanban, a whiteboard, and a voice recording program.

I'm always tweaking what I am doing, attempting to match my actions with what keeps me in the Right Thinking process instead of falling into human personality quirks. It's a balancing act.

It takes time. It's a practice. So we might as well settle in and enjoy the process.

Your quality word list is going to guide you. These qualities are what is important to you. They are a representation of the essence of who you are.

Have you set an intent, goal, or to-do that doesn't fit your qualities?

Stop, check, and see. Don't pass go until you do. Adjust. Pay attention.

Remember the four ways to use your list? Review the "how to" in Chapter Eleven. Use them.

Doing this first will save heartbreak and time and keep you on your Right Intent track.

Let's see what Sally is up to now.

Sally's Right Action

After discovering the joy of practicing, Sally has become much more faithful about the Right Thinking steps.

However, reaching the step called Right Action both scared Sally and excited her.

Part of Sally wished that all she had to do was think about what she wanted using the Right Thinking steps.

After all, things had started to change even without doing much more than the homework assignments.

It would be so much easier to just imagine things getting better and not have to do anything.

On the other hand, Sally recognized that she was holding herself back from doing things she had always wanted to do.

And the more she practiced the Right Thinking steps, the more she felt like doing them.

Sally could feel ideas bubbling around inside of her. It was both terrifying and exhilarating to realize that she was finally going to do something about them.

Now that Sally could recognize the difference between resisting what isn't true and resisting what she wanted to do, the action part of herself was raring to go.

All she had to do was get past the old version of herself, the old perceptions, the old hangups. She had to keep telling the voice in her head to shut up, and she often pictured shoving it behind a door and locking it.

Being persistent in denying what it was telling her helped a great deal and doing the I Choose sheets and Quality Word lists helped make it all much better.

Getting out of her own way made things so much easier. Just wishing and wanting had not worked. Taking Right Action was the solution.

The other thing that Sally was experiencing was a renewed desire to do things she had long ago forgotten she liked to do. It was interesting to Sally that although these things didn't specifically relate to her intent to get her health back, they made her feel better.

So Sally resolved to take action on the things that were calling her to do. In the process, she was happier with everyone around her.

Sally stopped blaming them for how she felt or how she looked. She hadn't even realized she had been doing that.

Once she realized that she had been blaming

others for where she was her in her life, Sally stopped by reminding herself who she was—a reflection of Love—which meant that the person who was annoying her was also a reflection of Love. *That is Right Reasoning,* Sally told herself.

The habit she worked on the most was the habit of feeling guilty or ashamed of how she had behaved, or what she hadn't done with her life, or how she had given up on her dreams.

That kind of thinking was not Right Thinking.

Sally realized that only by staying with Right Thinking could she clean up the messes she made and move happily forward in her life.

Sally took just one idea that had been bubbling up and made a goal and to-do list for it. It was easy now that she understood the difference between intent and a goal.

Yes, her intent remained to get her health back. She changed the wording, though. Now that she understood the process better, she realized what she wanted was to experience health. So that was her new intent.

Sally had always wanted to walk or run one of her town's charity events. So she made it a goal to walk in the next event and to finish. Someday she wanted to run it, but for now, this was a goal she knew she could accomplish.

Next, she made a list of action steps—things to do. Register for the walk was first on the list. Then she added stuff she would need. And how much she would walk every day to prepare.

As Sally finished up her seven weeks of Right Thinking, she realized that she could run through the seven steps in a flash, and in doing so, she could often heal a situation or problem quickly.

The day she and her husband started arguing, she silently walked herself through the Seven Steps.

This is what she said to herself.

I don't want to argue.
My intent is to stop this argument.
My premise is that Love is present here and now.
We are both expressions of love and wisdom.
I won't accept that he is wrong and I am right.
We are both just trying to be happy.
Yes, we are both expressions of love and wisdom.

With that, Sally reached out and touched his hand and smiled at him.

He sputtered to a stop and smiled back. And that was the end of the argument.

Yes, Sally decided. *Right Thinking does work.*

Here are Sally's seven steps for Right Thinking:

Overall Right Intent: *Experience health.*
Right Intent: *To feel better.*
Right Premise: *I am already healthy and I feel great*
Right Identity: *I am the expression of health*
Right Resistance: *I resist ungodly temptations.*
Right Reasoning: *I am not the human picture.*
Right Practice: *I practice with my quality words.*
Right Action: *I take action towards my dreams.*

Practical Action

As you finish up these seven weeks, keep the practice going.

You will get better and better at it and probably run through the steps in a flash.

Still, sometimes it helps to take all this time to work through something.

Don't be surprised if it changes and heals more things than what you began with.

What appears as a problem is a symptom. Doing these seven steps reveals the underlying issue and shifts it, thereby resolving the problem.

Step Seven: Right Action

My overall intent for reading this book:

My Right Intent:

My Right Premise:

My Right Identity:

My Right Resistance:

My Right Reasoning:

My Right Practice:

My Right Action:

Yes, you could continue with these practice steps if you wish.

• Continue noticing how you are self identifying, and how others see you.

- Keep your I Choose sheets going for anything that you are working on.

- Use your Quality Word lists to make decisions and shift perceptions.

- Choose at least one way that you will calm your thinking, quiet your mind and bring it into harmony with your intent. Do a meditation. Walk by yourself. Sit in nature. Listen to bird songs. Breathe.

ACTION REVIEW

Look back of these last seven weeks just one more time and answer these questions for yourself.

Things I noticed:

Ways I am stuck:

Things that have changed:

Chapter Thirteen: Recap

If you follow your bliss, doors will open for you that wouldn't have opened for anyone else." —Joseph Campbell

If you have gotten this far, you have already experienced the results of Right Thinking. Healing of some kind has taken place in your life.

Perhaps it wasn't what you thought you wanted to heal. Maybe it doesn't feel the way you thought it would. But something has happened.

It had to. We have shifted our thinking towards infinite possibilities and away from the limited worldview. That will always, always change our experience.

All we have to do is to be willing to experience it.

Perception blindness is a real thing. It's what we have been striving to clear up. To open our eyes to see the perfection already present.

Sometimes that perception blindness is due to conscious choices. Other times it's because we are stuck in what we think is happening or should happen.

This summer, I watched a row of dahlias as they grew. I had been lazy and not taken the roots out of the ground for the winter, and didn't expect them to return. However, we had a mild winter, and some of them had survived.

At the end of the summer, the dahlias bloomed, except for one huge one that kept getting bigger and bigger. I had never seen such a huge dahlia. Was it using all its energy to grow big, and that's why there were no blooms?

I asked myself that question for a few weeks. Then one day, I asked myself if it was really a dahlia. Just because it was growing where I planted one didn't mean it was one.

With that question, I realized that not only was it not a dahlia; it was a tree. Yes, a tree. I had trimmed it as if it was a dahlia, so it was multi-branched, but it was a tree.

Because I wasn't expecting a tree to be there, and because in the beginning, the leaves resembled dahlia leaves, and it was not a tree I had ever seen before, and because I wanted it to be a dahlia, it took months to see what was there all along.

I could tell you many stories about perception blindness. I am sure you could, too. We look for what we think the object or idea, looks like and not for its essence. And because of that, we don't see what is right in front of us.

Right in front of us is the perfection of the One Creator, the One creation. Right in front of us is the Truth of our Spiritual nature.

Blaming ourselves for not seeing it only makes it worse. Move forward. Look at what didn't work, only to move forward. Don't stay in the past. Learn from it and move forward.

Turn your attention to shifting out of perception blindness and into the light.

Then what appears to be broken or hurting or separated is more clearly seen in its Divine perfection. That's when we experience what we call healing.

Make an Intent to understand the Divine, to be Love in action. Be willing to let go of the human ego and personalities. They get in the way.

Like the tinman, the lion, the scarecrow, and Dorothy, we already have all we need. Use this thoughtful system of Right Thinking to find that out for yourself.

May our hearts be filled with the joy of Divine discovery. Strengthen us all to withstand that which ties us to the human beliefs of lack and limitation. May we all experience our true spiritual nature and light up the world with the awareness that we are One.

Here's a practice that may help.

Right Intent: *To live as the expression of the Divine.*
Right Premise: *I am the expression of the Divine.*
Right Identity: *I am Love Loving Itself.*
Right Reasoning: *Omnipotent God is Love.*
Right Resistance: *I resist anything that is not Love.*
Right Practice: *I consistently stay within the Truth.*
Right Action: *I do what Angel Ideas lead me to do.*

Author Note:

As I mentioned, this book is part of *The Shift Series.*

If you love the concepts and want to learn more about them, you will find them laid out in different ways in the other books.

Not all of them are workbooks like this one, but they are all practical.

When you join my mailing list, I'll give you a free book.

Join me here: becalewis.com

I am looking forward to getting to know you!

Beca

Here's *The Shift Series* **current list:**

- *Living in Grace*: The Shift to Spiritual Perception
- *The 4 Essential Questions*: Choosing Spiritually Healthy Habits
- *The 28 Day Shift To Wealth*: A Daily Prosperity Plan
- *The Intent Course*: Say Yes To What Moves You
- *The Daily Shift*: Daily Lessons From Love To Money
- *Imagination Mastery:* A Workbook For Shifting Your Reality
- *Seven Steps To Right Thinking:* A Thoughtful System for Healing

Coming Fall 2021: *Shift Your Perception:* Change Your Life

ACKNOWLEDGMENTS

My heartfelt thanks to the *Seven Step To Right Thinking* class for being the beta testers for this book.

And for those wonderful members of the Beca Book Community who encourage me to keep writing.

Thank you especially to Jet Tucker, Jamie Lewis, and Diana Cormier for cleaning up all my errors in this book, and always being there when I need them to check up on me.

More Ways To Connect:

Connect with me online:

http://www.facebook.com/becalewiscreative
https://www.facebook.com/groups/becalewisfans/
http://instagram.com/becalewis
http://www.linkedin.com/in/becalewis
https://www.goodreads.com/BecaLewis
http://www.pinterest.com/theshift/
http://www.twitter.com/becalewis
http://www.facebook.com/becalewis

ABOUT BECA LEWIS

Beca writes books that she hopes will change people's perceptions of themselves and the world, and open possibilities to things and ideas that are waiting to be seen and experienced.

At sixteen, Beca founded her own dance studio. Later, she received a Master's Degree in Dance in Choreography from UCLA and founded the Harbinger Dance Theatre, a multimedia dance company, while continuing to run her dance school.

After graduating—to better support her three children—Beca switched to the sales field, where she worked as an employee and independent contractor to many industries, excelling in each while perfecting and teaching her Shift® system, and writing books.

She joined the financial industry in 1983 and became an Associate Vice President of Investments at a major stock brokerage firm, and was a licensed Certified Financial Planner for more than twenty years.

This diversity, along with a variety of life challenges, helped fuel the desire to share what she's learned by writing and talking with the hope that it will make a difference in other people's lives.

Beca grew up in State College, PA, with the dream of becoming a dancer and then a writer. She carried that dream forward as she fulfilled a childhood wish by moving to Southern California in 1969. Beca told her family she would never move back to the cold.

After living there for thirty years, she met

her husband Delbert Lee Piper, Sr., at a retreat in Virginia, and everything changed. They decided to find a place they could call their own which sent them off traveling around the United States. For a year or so they lived and worked in a few different places before returning to live in the cold once again near Del's family in a small town in Northeast Ohio, not too far from State College.

When not working and teaching together, they love to visit and play with their combined family of eight children and five grandchildren, read, study, do yoga or taiji, feed birds, work in their garden, and design things. Actually, designing things is what Beca loves to do. Del enjoys the end result.

Made in the USA
Las Vegas, NV
21 March 2021